I0491728

TABLE OF CONTENTS

ABOUT THIS BOOK

Forex Trading contains the information you need to take the first step in trading the world's currencies:

Chapter 1: What is the Forex Market? It presents the global forex market and gives an idea of its size and scope.

Chapter 2: The Mechanics of Currency Trading observes how currencies are traded in the foreign exchange market: what currency pairs are exchanged, what price quote implies, how profits and losses are calculated, and how the global trading day flows.

Chapter 3: How to Develop a Profitable Forex Trading Mindset analyzes the different approaches used by professional currency traders to develop a profitable mindset.

Chapter 4: Getting Started Along with Your Practice Account guides you through the different ways you can establish a market position, how to manage your transaction during the open, how to close your position, and how to critically evaluate your results.

Chapter 5: Choosing Your Trading Style reviews the different approaches used by expert currency traders and how they impact trading decisions, as well as how to craft a disciplined trading plan and stick to it.

The second part of the book **(chapters 6 to 10)** deals more with the following topics:

- Basic Forex Strategies
- Brokers to avoid
- Dealing with loss
- Techniques to earn $ 15,000 per month in 2021
- Strategies for creating passive income with cryptocurrencies

CHAPTER ONE - WHAT IS FOREX MARKET?

The foreign exchange market - usually called the forex market, or simply refer to as the FX market - is the commonly traded financial market in the globe. We like to see the foreign exchange market as the "Big Kahuna" of the financial markets. The foreign exchange market is the crossroads of international capital, the crossroads through which global trade and investment flows must move. International trade flows, like when a Swiss electronics company buys components made in Japan, were originally the basis for the development of foreign exchange markets.

Today, however, the global investment and financial flows dominate trade as the main non-speculative source of foreign exchange market volume. Whether it is an Australian pension fund that invests in US Treasury bonds or a British insurer that allocates assets on the Japanese stock market or a German conglomerate that buys a Canadian-made facility, every international transaction goes through the foreign exchange market at some point.

More than anything, the foreign exchange market is a commercial market. It's a 24/7 market, allowing traders to act on news and events as they see fit. It's a market where half a billion dollars can be executed in a matter of seconds and may not even move prices in a remarkable way. Try to buy or sell half a billion products in another market and see how prices react.

GETTING INSIDE THE NUMBERS

The average daily volume of currency trading exceeds $ 2 trillion per day. That's an impressive number, right? $ 2,000,000,000 - it's a lot of zeros, no matter how you cut them. To give you such a perspective, it's about 10 to 15 times the size of the daily trading volume on all the stock markets of the world together.

SPECULATING IN THE CURRENCY MARKET

Although commercial and financial transactions on the money markets represent huge nominal amounts, they remain pale compared to values based on speculation. The vast majority of currency market volume is by far speculative - traders who buy and sell for short-term gains based on minute-to-minute, hour-to-hour, and day-to-day price fluctuations.

It is assessed that more than 90% of daily trading volume is derived from speculation (i.e., investment-based foreign exchange transactions or transactions represent less than 10% of the daily trading volume). The breadth and depth of the speculative market mean that the liquidity of the global currency market is unmatched among global financial markets.

Most spot currency trading, about 75 percent by volume, takes place in so-called "major currencies," which represent the largest and most developed economies in the world. In addition, foreign exchange activity often operates on the basis of the regional "currency bloc," where most of the negotiations take place between the USD block, the JPY block, and the EUR block, representing the three largest economic regions. world.

GETTING LIQUID WITHOUT GETTING SOAKED

Liquidity is known as the level of market interest - the buying and selling volume - available at any time for a particular security or asset. The greater the liquidity or, the deeper the trade, the easier and faster it is to buy or sell a security.

From a business perspective, liquidity is a critical consideration as it determines the speed at which prices move between trades and over time. A very liquid market such as forex can see large volumes of traded trades with relatively low price changes. A non-liquid or weak market tends to see prices rise faster in relatively lower trading volumes. A market that trades only for certain hours (futures, for example) also represents a less liquid and thinner market.

AROUND THE GLOBE IN A TRADING DAY

The forex market is active and opens 24 hours a day, from the opening hours on Monday morning in Asia-Pacific to the closing hours on Friday in New York. At any given time, according to the time zone, dozens of global financial centers - such as London. Sydney, or Tokyo - is open, and the exchange offices of these financial centers are active in the market.

Currency trading does not stop even on holidays, when other financial markets, such as stocks or futures exchanges, can be closed. Even if it is a vacation in Japan, for example, Sydney, Singapore, and Hong Kong can always be open. It may be July 4th in the United States, but if it's a business day, Tokyo, London, Toronto, and other financial centers will continue to trade currencies. The only common holiday in the world is New Year's Day, and even that depends on the day of the week it falls.

THE OPENING OF THE TRADING WEEK

There is no officially designated start time for the trading day or week, but for all intents and purposes, market action begins when Wellington, New Zealand, the first financial center to the west from the international data line, opens Monday morning, a local hour. Depending on if daylight saving time is in effect in its own time zone, it is approximately the beginning of Sunday afternoon in North America, Sunday night in Europe, and early Monday morning in Asia.

Sunday's opening is the starting point for a recovery in money markets after Friday's closing in North America (5 pm ET). This is the currency market's first chance to react to news and events that may have occurred over the weekend. Prices may have closed trades in New York at one level, but depending on the circumstances, they may start trading at different levels on open Sunday.

Trading In The Asia-Pacific Session

Trading volumes of currencies in the Asia-Pacific session represent about 21% of the world's total daily volume, according to a 2004 survey. The main centers business are Wellington, New Zealand; Sydney, Australia; Tokyo, Japan; Hong Kong; and Singapore. In terms of the most traded currency pairs, this means that news and data reports from New Zealand, Australia, and Japan will come to the market during this session.

Due to the size of the Japanese market and the importance of Japanese data in the market, much of the trade during the Asia-Pacific session focuses on Japanese Yen currency pairs (explained in more detail in Chapter 2), for example, USD / JPY - forex. to the US dollar / Japanese yen - and the JPY crosses, such as EUR / JPY and AUD / JPY. Of course, Japanese financial institutions are also more active during this session, so you can often understand what the Japanese market is doing based on price movements.

For individual traders, overall liquidity in major currency pairs is more than adequate, with generally orderly price movements. In some less liquid non-regional currencies such as GBP / USD or USD / CAD, price movements may be more irregular or non-existent depending on the environment.

Trading in the European/London session

In the middle of the Asian session, European financial centers are starting to open the market and are booming. The center's European   financial account and London for over 50% of the total daily volume of world trade, with London representative alone for about a third of the total daily global volume, according to the survey in 2004.

The European session spans half of the Asian trade and half of the US trade, which means that market interest and liquidity peak in this session.

Current events and data from the euro area (and from countries such as Germany and France), Switzerland, and the United Kingdom are generally reported in the early hours of the European session. As a result, some of the most active and largest active deals are in European currencies (EUR, GBP, and CHF) and cross currency pairs (EUR / CHF and EUR / GBP).

The Asian trading centers are beginning to slow down in the early hours of the European session in the morning, and US financial centers arrive a few hours later, about 7 am Brasilia time.

Trading In The North American Session

Due to the overlap between the US and European trading sessions, trading volumes are much larger. Some of the largest and most important directional price movements occur during this transition period. In itself, however, the US trading session is about the same share of world trade volume in the Asia-Pacific market, about 22% of the world's daily trading volume.

The American morning is the time when the main US economic data are released, and the foreign exchange market makes many of its most important decisions on the value of the dollar. Most US data reports are published at 8:30 am ET, while others are published later (between 9am and 10am ET). Canadian data reports are also published in the morning, usually between 7 am and 9 am Brasilia time. There are also US economic reports that come out at noon or 2 pm ET, animating the New York market afternoon. London and the Centers European financial start to close their daily trading operations at noon Eastern Time (ET) each day. London, or the closure of Europe, as we know, can often generate volatile business upheavals.

Most days, the liquidity and interest rates drop significantly in the afternoon of New York, which can lead to difficult trading conditions. In calm weather, a general decline in market interest often leads to stagnation of price action. On more active days, when prices may have changed more significantly, a decline in liquidity may trigger additional excessive price movements as fewer traders strive for similar prices and liquidity. As with the closing of London, there is never a precise way to move the New York afternoon market, so traders need to be aware that lower liquidity conditions tend to prevail and that adapt accordingly.

CURRENCIES AND SOME FINANCIAL MARKETS

As much as we like to refer to the forex market as a whole and at the end of all financial markets, it does not exist in a vacuum. You may have even heard of some of these other markets: gold, oil, stocks, and bonds.

There are several misinformation and noise about the supposed interdependence between these markets and individual currencies or currency pairs. To be sure, you can still find a correlation between two different markets over a period of time, even if it is just zero (i.e., the two markets are not correlated).

Always remember that all the different financial markets are markets in their own right and operate according to their internal dynamics based on feelings, data, news, and positioning. Do the markets sometimes overlap and have different degrees of correlation? Of course, and it's always important to know what's happening in other financial markets. But it is also essential to consider each market from its own point of view and to negotiate each market individually.

Let's dive into some of the other major financial markets and see what conclusions we can draw for currency trading.

Gold

Gold is commonly known as a hedge against inflation, an alternative to the US dollar, and a store of value in the period of political or economic uncertainty. In the long run, the relationship is almost reversed, with a weaker dollar generally accompanying a higher gold price and a stronger dollar accompanying a lower gold price. However, in the short term, each market has its own dynamics and liquidity, which makes short-term trading relationships generally fragile.

Overall, the gold market is much smaller than the foreign exchange market, so if we were gold traders, we would keep an eye on what is happening with the dollar, not the other way around. With this observed, extreme movements in gold prices tend to grab the attention of currency traders and generally influence the dollar upside down.

Oil

There are tons of wrong information on the internet about the supposed relationship between oil and the US dollar or other currencies such as CAD or JPY. The idea is that, as some countries are oil producers, their currencies are positively (or negatively) affected by increases (or decreases) in oil prices. If the country is an oil importer (and which countries are not today?), The theory is that your currency will be affected (or aided) by higher (or lower) oil prices.

Correlation studies show no appreciable relationships in this sense, especially in the short term, which is central to most trading currencies. When there is a long-term relationship, it is as obvious to the dollar as one or more than any single currency, whether it is an importer or an exporter of black gold .

The most effective way to look at oil is as an inflation factor and a limiting factor in overall economic development. The greater the price of oil, the higher the inflation, and the more likely the economy will slow down. The lesser the price of oil, the less inflationary pressures are likely (but not necessarily). We like to take into account changes in oil prices in our expectations of inflation and growth, and then draw conclusions about the evolution of the dollar. Above all, oil is just one of many.

Stock

Equities are microeconomic bonds, which rise and fall in response to the results and prospects of individual firms, while currencies are essentially macroeconomic bonds, fluctuating in response to broader economic and political developments. As such, there are few intuitive reasons for equity markets to be linked to currencies. Long-term correlation studies confirm this, with essentially zero correlation coefficients between major US pairs and US equity markets over the last five years.

The two markets sometimes intersect, although this usually occurs only at extremes and for very short periods. For example, when stock market volatility reaches extraordinary levels (for example, Standard & Poor's loses more than 2% in one day), the dollar may be subject to more pressure than otherwise - but there is no guarantee. The US stock market may have fallen into an unexpected rise in US interest rates, while the US dollar may rise with the surprise action.

Bond

Bond markets or fixed income have a more intuitive link with the foreign exchange market because both are strongly influenced by interest rate expectations. However, the dynamics of short-term market supply and demand disrupt most attempts to establish a viable link between the two markets in the short term. Sometimes, the foreign exchange market reacts first and faster, depending on the evolution of interest rate expectations. At most times, the bond market more accurately shows changes in interest rate expectations as the currency market bounces back later.

Overall, as currency traders, you should definitely keep an eye on the benchmark returns of major currency countries to better track the expectations of the interest rate market. Changes in interest rates (interest rate differentials) have a major influence on foreign exchange markets.

The forex market possesses its own set of trading conventions and the associated language, just like any financial market. If you are new to currency trading, mechanics and terminology may take a while to get used to. But in the end, most currency trading conventions are quite simple.

BUYING AND SELLING SIMULTANEOUSLY

The biggest mental barrier that newcomers face in currencies, especially those in many other markets, is that each transaction consists of a simultaneous purchase and sale. On the stock market, for example, if you buy 100 shares of Google, you have 100, and you expect to see the price increase. When you want to get out of this position, you are simply selling what you bought previously. Easy no?

But in currencies, the purchase of currency involves the simultaneous sale of another currency. This is the exchange of foreign currency. Succinctly put, if you are looking for a rise in the dollar, the question is "bigger against what?"

The answer is another motto. In relative terms, if the dollar appreciates against another currency, this other currency will also fall against the dollar. If you think about it in stock market terms, when you buy a stock, you sell money, and when you sell a stock, you buy money.

CURRENCIES COME IN PAIRS

To make matters easier, the exchange markets refer to currencies traded in pairs, with names that combine the two different currencies exchanged or "traded" against each other.

In addition, the currency markets have given nicknames or abbreviations to most currency pairs, which refer to the pair and not necessarily to the different currencies involved.

Major currency pairs

The main currency pairs involve the US dollar on one side of the business. The main currency denominations are expressed using the International Organization for Standardization (ISO) codes for each currency. Table 2-1 lists the most traded currency pairs, what they are called in conventional terms, and what nicknames gave them the market.

Table 2-1	The Major U.S. Dollar Currency Pairs		
ISO Currency Pair	**Countries**	**Long Name**	**Nickname**
EUR/USD	Eurozone*/U.S.	Euro-dollar	N/A
USD/JPY	U.S./Japan	Dollar-yen	N/A
GBP/USD	United Kingdom/U.S.	Sterling-dollar	Sterling or Cable
USD/CHF	U.S./Switzerland	Dollar-Swiss	Swissy
USD/CAD	U.S./Canada	Dollar-Canada	Loonie
AUD/USD	Australia/U.S.	Australian-dollar	Aussie or Oz
NZD/USD	New Zealand/U.S.	New Zealand-dollar	Kiwi

* The Eurozone is made up of all the countries in the European Union that have adopted the euro as their currency.

Major cross-currency pairs

While the vast majority of currency trading takes place in pairs of dollars, cross-currency pairs serve as an alternative to always trading the US dollar. A cross-currency pair, or *cross* or *cross* for short, is a currency pair that does not include the US dollar. Crossed rates are derived from the respective dollar pairs, but are quoted independently.

Crosses allow traders to direct trades more directly to specific individual currencies to make the most of events and news.

For instance, your analysis may propose that the Japanese yen has the worst outlook for all current major currencies, based on interest rates or economic prospects. To take advantage of it, you want to sell JPY, but against what another motto? You are considering the USD, potentially buying USD / JPY (buying USD / selling JPY), but then concluding that the USD outlook is not much better than JPY. Future research from you could point to another currency with much better prospects (such as high or rising interest rates or signs of strengthening the economy), says the Australian dollar (AUD). In this example, you would try to buy the AUD / JPY cross for your opinion that AUD has the best prospects between the major currencies and the worst JPY.

The most vigorously traded crosses focus on the three major currencies other than the USD (i.e., EUR, JPY, and GBP) and are called Euro Crosses, Yen Crosses, and Sterling Crosses. Table 2-2 presents the most actively traded cross currency pairs.

Table 2-2	Most Actively Traded Cross Pairs	
ISO Currency Pair	*Countries*	*Market Name*
EUR/CHF	Eurozone/Switzerland	Euro-Swiss
EUR/GBP	Eurozone/United Kingdom	Euro-sterling
EUR/JPY	Eurozone/Japan	Euro-yen
GBP/JPY	United Kingdom/Japan	Sterling-yen
AUD/JPY	Australia/Japan	Aussie-yen
NZD/JPY	New Zealand/Japan	Kiwi-yen

THE LONG AND THE SHORT OF IT

Foreign exchange markets make use of the same terms to express the market positioning of most other financial markets. But as currency trading involves simultaneous buying and selling, clarity of terms helps - especially if you are completely new to the financial market.

Going long

No, we are not talking about running away for a football pass. A long position, or simply a long position, refers to a position in the market in which you purchased security. In foreign currency means the purchase of a currency pair. When you buy, you are looking for higher prices in order to sell at a higher price than what you purchase. When you decide to close a long position, you have to sell what you bought. If you shop at different price levels, you increase the lengths, and you get longer.

Getting short

A short, or simply a short position, refers to a position in the market in which you sold a stock you never owned. On the stock market, selling short stocks requires you to borrow stock (and pay a fee to the loan broker) before you can sell it. In the currency markets, this means that you have sold a currency pair, which means that you sold the base currency and bought the counter currency. You make so always an exchange, only in reverse order and according to the listing requirements of the currency pair. When you trade a currency pair, it's called a short sale or a short sale, and that means you're looking for the price of the pair to go down so you can buy it in a profitable way. If you sell at different price levels, you add shorts, and you shorten.

In currency trading, shorts are as common in the long run. "Sell high and buy low" is a standard currency trading strategy.

Currency pair rates show relative values between two currencies, not the absolute price of a single stock or commodity. Since currencies can fall or increase in relation to each other in medium and long-term trends and minute-by-minute fluctuations, currency pair prices are likely to fall at any time. To take advantage of these movements, foreign investors often use short positions to exploit the fall in currency prices. Traders in other markets may feel ill at ease with the sales out, but it is something you must understand.

Squaring up

To have no position in the market is called a square or a flat. If you have an open position and want to close it, it's called square. If you are small, you must buy to make a square. If you are long, you will have to sell to stay stable. The only time you have no exposure to the market or financial risk is when you are up to date.

23

PROFITS AND LOSSES

Profit and Loss (P & L) is the way traders measure failure and success. A clear understanding of how Profit & Loss works are particularly critical for online margin trading, where your Profit & Loss directly affects the amount of margin you need to work with. Changes to your margin balance determine how much you can trade and how much time you can trade if prices change against you.

MARGIN BALANCES AND LIQUIDATIONS

When opening an online currency trading account, you will have to pay money as collateral to meet the margin requirements set by your dealer. This initial margin deposit becomes your opening margin balance and is the basis on which all your subsequent transactions are guaranteed. Unlike futures markets or margin-based stock trading, online forex brokers do not issue margin calls (requests for additional collateral to support open positions). Instead, they establish margin balance indices for open positions that must be upheld at all times.

Here's an instance to help you understand how the required margin indices work. Suppose you have an account with a leverage ratio of 100: 1 (so that a $ 1 margin in your own account can control a $ 100 position size), but your broker requires a 100% margin rate, which means you have to maintain 100% of the required margin at any time. The ratio varies depending on the size of the account, but a 100% margin requirement is typical for small accounts. This means that to have a $ 10,000 position size, you will need $ 100 in your account because when you divide $ 10,000 by the leverage ratio of $ 100 is $ 100. If your account margin falls below the required rate, your broker is probably entitled to terminate your positions without notice. If your broker liquidates your position, it usually means that your losses are blocked, and your margin balance has become smaller.

Make sure you understand your broker's margin requirements and settlement policies. The requirements may differ depending on the size of the account and whether you are negotiating mini lot sizes (10,000 units) or standard lot sizes (100,000 currency units). Some broker settlement policies allow you to liquidate all positions if you do not meet the margin requirements. Others close the most significant losses or parts of losses until the required proportion is satisfied again. You can find the details in the small print of the account opening contract that you sign. Always went through the fine print to ensure you understand the margins and trade policies of your broker.

UNREALIZED AND REALIZED PROFIT AND LOSS

Most online forex brokers provide real-time valuation calculations showing your margin balance. Mark-to-market is the calculation that shows unrealized results based on where you can close your open positions in the market at that time. Depending on your broker's market platform, if you are long, the calculation will usually be based on where you could sell at that time. If you are small, the price used will be the one where you can buy at that time. Your margin balance is the total sum of your unrealized profit, your initial margin deposit, and your realized profit.

The realized P & L is what you get when you close a trade position or part of a trade position. If you close the full position and become stable, everything you have done or lost will disappear from the unrealized profit calculation and will enter your margin balance. If you close only a portion of your open positions, only this portion of the trading result is realized and enters the margin balance. Your unrealized profit continues to fluctuate based on the remaining open positions, as well as the balance of the total margin.

If you have an open winning position, your unrealized profit is positive, and your margin balance increases. If the market changes relative to your positions, your unrealized result is negative, and your margin balance is reduced. Forex prices change constantly, so the result of your mark-to-market and the balance of the total margin also change constantly.

Calculation of profit and loss with pips

Profit and loss calculations are quite simple in terms of mathematics - all based on the size of the position and the number of pips you make or lose. A pip is the smallest increase in currency price fluctuations . The glitches can also be called points; we use both terms interchangeably.

Examining certain currency pairs helps you get an idea of what a pip is. Most currency pairs are quoted by making use of five digits. The appointment of the decimal point depends on whether it is a JPY currency pair; In this case, there are two digits behind the decimal point. All other currency pairs have four digits behind the decimal point. In all cases, this last figure is the pip.

Here are some of the main currency pairs and crosses, with the pip underlined:

EUR / USD: 1.2853

USD / CHF: 1.2267

USD / JPY: 117.23

EUR / JPY: 150.65

Focus first on the EUR / USD price. Looking at EUR / USD, if the price went from 1.2885 to 1.2873, it went up 20 pips. If it goes from 1.2853 to 1.2792, it drops by 61 pips. The glitches make it easy to calculate the results. To turn this pip movement into a profit and loss calculation, all you need to know is the size of the position. For a position of 100 000 EUR / USD, the movement of 20 pip equals $ 200 (100,000 EUR × 0.0020 = 200 $). For a position of 50,000 EUR / USD, the 61-point movement translates to $ 305 (50,000 EUR × 0.0061 = $ 305).

Whether the values are negative or positive depends on whether you were long or short for each movement. If you were small for the highest blow, it's a - in front of $ 200, if you were long, it was a +. EUR / USD is not difficult to calculate, especially for USD-based traders, because the result is accumulated in US dollars.

If you use USD / CHF, you will need to do another calculation before understanding the meaning. Indeed, the result will be denominated in Swiss francs (CHF), because CHF is the counter-currency. If the USD / CHF goes from 1.22267 to 1.2233 and you have less than $ 100,000 for the lowest movement, you just get a 34-pips drop. This is a profit of CHF 340 ($ 100,000 × 0.0034 = CHF 340). Yes, but how much does it represent in real money? To convert to USD, you must divide CHF 340 by the USD / CHF rate. Use the closing rate of transactions

(1.2233) because that's the position of the market the last time, and you get $ 277.94.

Even the venerable pip is being updated as e-commerce continues to grow. A few paragraphs ago, we say that pip is the smallest increase in currency price fluctuations. Not so fast. The online market is growing rapidly to decimal pips (trading at 1/10 pips), and half-pip prices have been the norm in some inter-bank currency pairs for many years.

Factoring profit and loss on margin calculations

The great news is that online FX trading platforms automatically calculate the outcome for you, both unrealized when trading is open and when trading is closed. So why did we just drag it through a mathematical calculation of results using pips? As online brokers, do not start calculating your result for you until after you complete a transaction.

To structure your trading and effectively manage your risk (what is the size of a position, what is the margin of risk?), You will have to calculate your P & L results before entering the trade.

Understanding the P & L implications of a trading strategy you are considering is essential to maintaining your margin balance and keeping control of your transactions. This simple exercise can help you avoid costly mistakes, such as making very large transactions or placing stop-loss orders beyond price when your account falls below the margin requirement. At a minimum, you must calculate the price at which your position will be settled when your margin balance falls below the required rate.

UNDERSTANDING ROLLOVERS AND INTEREST RATES

An exclusive market convention for foreign currencies scrolls. A rollover is a transaction in which an open position from a value date (settlement date) is postponed to the next value date. Rollovers represent the intersection of interest rate and currency markets.

After all, the currency is money.

The turnover rates are based on the difference in interest rates of the two currencies of the pair you are trading. This is because what you really exchange is good old-fashioned money. When you have a long currency, it's like having a bank deposit. If you have a short currency, it's like borrowing a loan. Just as you expect to earn interest on a bank deposit or pay interest on a loan, you should expect a gain / interest charge to maintain a foreign currency position on the change in value.

Consider an open currency position as an account with a positive balance (the currency you buy) and one with a -ve balance (the currency you buy). However, as your accounts are in two different currencies, the two interest rates for different countries apply.

The difference between interest rates in both countries is called the interest rate differential. The higher the interest rate differential, the greater the impact of bearings. The narrower the interest rate spread, the lower the effect of rollovers. You can find the relevant interest rate levels of major currencies on a number of financial markets sites. Look for basic or reference loan rates in each country.

Application of rollovers

Rollover transactions are usually done automatically by your forex broker if you hold an open position after the date of the change in value.

Overlaps are applied to your open position by two clearing operations that result in the same open position. Some online forex brokers apply scroll rates by adjusting the average rate of your open position. Other forex brokers apply turnover rates by applying the credit or debit roll directly to your margin balance.

Understanding currency rates

Here we look at how online brokers display currency prices and what they mean for trading and order execution. Remember that different online forex brokers use different formats to display prices on their trading platforms.

Offers and Bids

When you are in front of the screen, and you are looking at the trading platform of an online forex broker, you will see two prices for each currency pair. The price on the left is called the offer, and the right price is called the offer (some call it asking). The bid is the cost at which you can trade the base currency. The "offer" is the cost at which you can buy the base currency.

Some brokers display prices on top of each other, with supply down and supply up. The simplest way to know the difference is that the offer price is always lower than the offer price.

The listing of each offer and offer you see will have two components: the overview and the trading price. The large figure refers to the first three digits of the overall exchange rate and is usually displayed in a smaller font size or even in the shadow. The negotiated price refers to the last two digits of the price of the general currency and is brilliantly displayed in larger font size.

Spreads

A difference is a difference between the bid price and the bid price. Most online forex brokers use spread-based trading platforms for individual traders. Look at the gap as the compensation that the broker receives to be the market maker and perform his trade.

The spreads vary from one broker to another and in currency pairs in each broker as well. As a general rule, the more liquid the currency pair, the smaller the spread; The less the currency pair is liquid, the larger the gap. This is particularly the case for some of the less traded passages.

CHAPTER THREE - HOW TO DEVELOP A PROFITABLE FOREX TRADING MINDSET

It is an inevitable reality that your success or failure in forex trading will largely depend on your state of mind. In other words, if your psychology of Forex trading is not correct, you will not earn money! Unfortunately, most dealers ignore this important fact or do not know how important it is to have an appropriate mindset for the success of Forex trading. If you do not have the right trading mentality, whatever the quality of your trading strategy, because no strategy will ever make cash if it is used by a professional with bad psychology.

Note: I would like to know how you plan to use the points discussed here to improve your Forex trading mindset. Leave me your comments and comments below after reading today's lesson!

Many people seem to be unaware that they are negotiating with a state of mind that stops them from making money in the markets. Instead, they think that if they find the right system or indicator, they will magically start printing money on their computers. Success in business is the end result of developing good business habits, and habits are the end result of good business psychology. Today's lesson will give you the information you need to develop a profitable business mindset; So read this lesson carefully and do not ignore it, because I promise you that the reason you are having problems in the markets is that your mindset works against you rather than for you.

Step 1: You must have realistic expectations

The first thing you must do to develop the right Forex trading mentality is to have realistic expectations of trading. I mean this; Do not think that you will leave your job and start earning $ 1 million a year after two months of live trading with your $ 5,000 account. It doesn't work this way, and the sooner you base your expectations, the sooner you start making money consistently. You must accept that you can not negotiate and leverage the path to business success. If you do both, you can make money fast, but you will soon lose everything and more. Accept the reality of the money you have on your trading account and the amount you are willing to lose by trading. Here are some other things to consider:

• **Trade only with disposable risk capital** - The **capital** disposable is money you do not need for your living expenses, including retirement and other long-term things. If you do not have capital available or risky, keep doing demos until you have, or stop trading together, but whatever you do, do not trade with money because you will be delighted of the loss. Always assume that you can lose the money you have on your account or in a trade ... if you really agree with that, then you should go, just make sure not to lie to you ... REALLY OK, Exchanging "scared" money (money you can not afford to lose) will cause intense emotional pressure and loss.

• **Make sure you can always sleep at night** - This is related to the point above about available capital. But the major difference is that you must ask EVERY transaction, whether you are 100% neutral or OK, with the possibility of losing the money you are about to risk. If you can not sleep at night because you think about your business, you risk doing too much. No one can dictate how much you risk in trading; it depends on how comfortable you are personally. If you trade 4 times per month, you can obviously risk a little more per transaction than someone who deals 30 times a month ... it's about your trading frequency, your skills as a trader, and your tolerance for personal risk.

• **Understand that each transaction is independent of the previous one -** This is important because I know that many traders are overly influenced by their previous trades. The fact is that your last company has absolutely nothing to do with your next business. You must avoid becoming euphoric or overconfident after a winning or vengeful negotiation after a lost negotiation. The fact is that every time you trade, this should only be considered as a new execution of your trading margin; If you only had three consecutive winners, avoid risking more than usual in your next exchange, simply because you feel very confident and avoid returning to the market immediately after a lost exchange, just to try What You Lost. When you do these things, you operate 100% with emotions rather than logic and objectivity.

• **Do not get too focused on your trades -** If you follow the three points we've just discussed, it's unlikely that you'll focus too much on your business. Do not take trades in person; it's not because you lose in a few trades in a row that you're bad at trading, even if you win in three trades in a row, it does not mean you're a negotiator "God" safe from losing. If you do not risk a lot by negotiating and do not trade with the money you

35

require for other things in your life, you are probably not very attached to your business.

Step 2: Understand the power of patience

I think one of the biggest achievements that allowed me to turn my own operations is that I did not have to trade a lot to get a decent monthly return. Think about it; most people consider an annual return of 6% is very good for an account of savings, and if you value your retirement fund to 12% per year, you are very happy. So, why do most traders expect 100% per month or some other unrealistic return? What is the problem of winning 5 or 10% per month? It's still exceptional over a year. Although I can not suggest that you make a certain percentage per month, if you understand that slower and more consistent profits are the path to long-term market success, you will be much better at the end of each year. negotiation. Here are some other things to consider about patience:

• **Learn how to trade on daily charts first** - By learning to trade first on daily chart periods, you will naturally take a broader approach to markets and avoid the temptation to over-trade. the delays induce. Beginning traders must especially slow down and learn to trade the daily charts first. Daily charts give the most practical and relevant view of the market. You do not have to trade every day to get a solid return every month.

• **Quality rather than quantity** - I consider myself a "sniper" on the market; I wait for days or even a week without negotiating when I see a price action parameter that triggers my alarm "it's obvious" ... I shoot the trigger with ZERO emotion. I am always ready to lose the money I risked in any profession because I negotiated that if I am 100% convinced that my room for negotiation on the price action is present.

Use Your Bullets Wisely - To truly harness the power of patience in developing the right business mindset, you need to understand that patience will instill you with positive business habits. Patience strengthens positive trading patterns, while emotional negotiation reinforces negative ones. Once you have begun to negotiate patiently, you will see how the judicious use of your "bullets" ... you just need a few good transactions a month to get a respectable return on the markets; Once you have it patiently, you will learn to appreciate NOT being in the markets ... because then you are "looking for prey." This contrasts with the frustrated and frustrated trader who stays up all night watching the graphics as a zombie who simply does not accept that he has to trade less often.

Step 3: Be ordered in your approach to the markets

You MUST have a business plan, a business journal, and you must plan the bulk of your stock market before you can enter. The more you plan before you register, the more likely you are to make money in the long run. You will ALWAYS interpret the market more precisely when you are not in business ... so planning everything increases your chances of making money because you work more on logic than on emotion.

• **Adopt a trading plan** - I know it can be boring, I know you might think you do not "need" to make one, but if you do not make a trading plan and you really use and adjust as you learn, you will start to negotiate in a disorganized and possibly emotional way. A business plan should not be a very dry and boring document; You can be creative with that. Your trading plan may be that you write your own weekly comment before the start of each week, plan what you will do and look for next week ... just make sure you have a "plan of attack" already before you begin all trading.

• **Keep a professional trading log** - You need a history, you have to record your transactions, you must do it in a forex trading journal. This is an essential element to forge the right Forex trading mentality as it provides a tangible document that you can view and instantly get rough feedback on the performance of your trading. Once you begin to keep a journal of your trades, it will become a habit, and you will not want to see any emotional results you look at in your corporate journal. Finally, you will see your trading diary as a work of art that proves your capability to trade with dignity as well as your capacity to follow your trading plan. This is something that any serious investor will want to see if he is considering trading other people's money.

• **Think before shooting, not after** - All the planning and pre-emption I just mentioned is akin to thinking before shooting. A weapon is a very powerful weapon, we all know we have to think before we shoot, even if we just hunt or shoot at close range. Similarly, markets can be very powerful "weapons" to win or lose money. So, you want to think as much as possible before starting a job, because once you enter, you will naturally become more emotional and will not want to be able to conclude pitiful transactions constantly. If you plan your actions before joining, you should not regret your operations, even when you lose trades. I never regret the exchanges I receive because I only negotiate if my advantage is present, and I am always comfortable with the amount of money I have risked in any transaction.

Step 4: Do not have doubts about your business advantage

Finally, do not start trading for real money if you do not know how to trade your advantage. Obviously, you will not develop the appropriate trading mindset if you enter the trading of an active account without being 100% sure of what you are looking for. Whatever your benefit, make sure you can redeem it on a demo account for at least three months or more before uploading it. Not just "dive" without feeling completely comfortable with your approach ... that's what most traders do, and most of them also lose money.

• **Have 100% confidence in your advantage -** I have 100% confidence in my price action trading strategies ... that does not mean I'm fool enough to believe that ALL trades will win, but I am completely confident that every time I negotiate my advantage is really present. I do not compromise my business advantage by making settings that seem "almost" good enough ... I just do not work in this case. I take only the price action patterns that I feel in my instincts as valid high-probability representations of my benefit. Therefore, I am never afraid or worried about the negotiations I enter, even if I lose.

• **Do not gamble -** There are skilled traders and people who play in the markets. If you take a calculated and calm approach to your trading and wait patiently for your trading margin to appear as a sniper, then you are a skilled trader. If you "run and shoot" and deviate from your trading plan, you are a player. So, are you a Foreign exchange trader or a player?

• **Price action trading helps develop an appropriate trading mindset -** My benefit is price action, and I am convinced that the simplicity of price share trading has helped me develop and maintain a mindset of proper Forex trading. We do not need tons of confusing indicators on our charts, and we do not need Forex trading robots or other expensive software. All we need is the raw action of market prices and our magnificent human spirit to interpret it; it is up to us to exploit this power.

The action on market prices gives us a map to follow, and of course, if we can ignore the emotional temptations that pop up in our minds, we will have no problem taking advantage of this price action card. I believe that today's lesson has provided some tips on how to develop the right mindset, ignore the emotions, and ditch the habits that destroy the success of your business.

CHAPTER FOUR – GETTING STARTED WITH YOUR PRACTICE ACCOUNT

The best way for beginners to understand currency trading is to open a practice account.

Almost all forex brokers offer a free practice account to potential customers; Simply register on the broker's website. The practice accounts are funded with "virtual" money, so you can do real money trading and gain experience with how margin trading works.

Practice Accounts give you an excellent opportunity to experience the Foreign exchange market. You can see how prices fluctuate at different times of the day, how different currency pairs may differ, and how the forex market reacts to new information when big news and economic data are released. You can also start trading in real market conditions without fear of losing money, trying different trading strategies to see how they work, acquire experience using different orders and manage open positions, improve your understanding of how trading and margin leverage. work and start by analyzing the graphs and following the technical indicators.

Practice accounts are a great way to get to know the Forex market closely and in person. They are also a great way to test all the features and functionality of a broker's platform. However, the only thing you can not simulate is the pleasure of managing real money. To get the most out of your practice account experience, treat your practice account as if it were real money.

PULLING THE TRIGGER

It's time to pull the trigger, buddy. This section assumes that you have registered for a practice account with an online forex broker and that you are ready to start some hands-on operations.

You trade on the foreign exchange market in two ways: you can trade *on the market* or at the current price using the click and auction function of your broker's platform, or you can use commands such as limited commands and commands with another cancellation (OCO).

CLICKING AND DEALING

Most traders like the idea of opening a trading position rather than leaving an order that may or may not be executed. They prefer to make sure they are on the market. Active buying and selling are also elements that make trading and speculation as fun as hard.

Most foreign exchange brokers provide live streaming prices that you can manage with a single click of your computer mouse. To trade on these platforms:

- **Specify the amount of trade you want to perform.**
- **Click the Buy or Sell button to carry out the operation.**

The forex trading platform responds, usually in one or two seconds, to let you know if the transaction has succeeded:

If the transaction is complete, you will receive a contextual confirmation of the platform, and your open list will be updated to reflect the new transaction.

If trading fails because the trading price has changed before receiving your request, you will receive a response stating "changed rates," "unavailable price," or something in that sense. You must repeat the steps to make a new trading attempt.

Sometimes attempts to trade on the market may fail in rapidly changing markets when prices adjust rapidly, for example, after the publication of data or the violation of a relevant technical level or price. Part of this stems from the *effect* of *the latency* Internet commerce, which refers to the delay in time between the price of the flat - form that comes to your computer and your trade request to the flat - form server.

If trading fails because trading was too much, depending on your margin, you will have to reduce the size of the trade.

Understand from the start that any action you take on a trading platform is your responsibility. You may want to click Buy instead of Sell, but no one knows for sure, except you.

USING ORDERS

Orders are essential trading tools in the foreign exchange market. Think of them as a company waiting for realization, because that's exactly what they are. If you enter an order and a successive price action triggers its execution, you will be in the market, so be very careful when placing your orders on the market.

Currency traders use orders to capture market movements when they are not in front of their screens. *Don't Forget:* the foreign exchange market is open 24 hours a day, five days a week. A change in the market is likely to occur while you sleep or shower while watching the screen. If you are a part-time trader, you will probably have a full-time job that requires attention when you are at work. (At least, your boss *expects* to *what* it retains your attention.) The orders are the way you can act on the market without being. Experienced Forex traders also regularly use orders to:

- Implement a business strategy from entry to exit
- Capture sudden fluctuations in short-term prices
- Limit risk in volatile or uncertain markets
- Preserve the commercial capital of unwanted losses
- Maintain commercial discipline
- Protect profits and minimize losses

We can not emphasize enough the importance of order in currency trading. Foreign exchange markets can be notoriously volatile and difficult to predict. The use of orders makes it possible to capitalize on short-term market movements by limiting the impact of any unfavorable price movement. While there is no guarantee that using orders will limit your losses or protect your profits in all market conditions, disciplined use of orders helps to quantify the risk you are taking and, with a little luck, gives you peace of mind. your negotiation. Bottom Line: If you do not use orders, you probably do not have a well-thought-out trading strategy - and it's a painful recipe.

Types of Orders

Several types of orders are available on the foreign exchange market. Remember that not all order types are available from all online brokers; therefore, add order types to the questions to ask your potential forex broker.

Take-profit orders

Do not you just like that name? An old market saying says, "You can not fail to make a profit." Use *profit orders* to make gains when you have an open position in the market. If you have a short USD / JPY at 117.20, your profit order would be to buy back the position and be somewhere below that price, for example, 116.80. If you buy GBP / USD at 1.8840, your profit order will be to sell the position somewhere higher, maybe 1.8875.

Limit orders

Limit orders are orders that trigger the trade-in levels more favorable than the price
of the *current* market. Think about buying low, selling high. If the limit order is to purchase, it must be entered at a price lower than the current market price. If the limit order is sold, it must be placed at a price higher than the current market price.

Stop-Loss Orders

Boo! The sound is bad, right? In fact, stop-loss orders are essential to the survival of trading. The traditional *stop-loss order* does exactly that: it stops losses by closing an open position that loses money. Make use of stop-loss orders to limit your losses if the market moves against your position. Otherwise, you leave for the market, which is dangerous.

Stop-loss orders are on a different side of the current price of profit orders, but in a similar direction (in terms of buying or selling). If you go long, your stop-loss order will sell, but at a price lower than the current market price. If you are small, your stop-loss order will purchase but at a higher price than the present market.

Trailing stop-loss orders

You may have been told that one of the keys to successful trading is to reduce lost positions and let winning positions run quickly. A final stop-loss order lets you do just that. The logic is that when you have a winning job, you expect the market to reverse and withdraw, instead of trying to choose the right level to get out of it.

A stop-loss order is a stop-loss order that you set to a fixed number of pips from your entry rate. The last stop adjusts the order rate as the market price changes, *but only in the direction of your transaction.* For example, if you bought EUR / CHF at 1.5750 and set the mobile stop at 30 pips, the stop will initially be activated at 1.5720 (1.5750-30 pips).

If the EUR / CHF price rises to 1.5760, the stop adjusts higher pip by pip with the price and is active on

1.5730. The trailing stop continues to adjust as the market continues to grow. When the market reaches the top, your last stop will be 30 pips (or the distance you specify) below that peak, wherever you are.

If the market drops by 30 pips, as in this example, your stop will be triggered, and your position will close. Therefore , in this case, if you have a time of 1.5750 and set a mobile stop of 30 pip, the shutdown becomes initially active at 1.5720. If the market never goes up and down, you will be stopped at

1.5720. If the price goes up first to 1.5775 then decreases by 60 points, your final stop will have increased to 1.5745 (1.5775-30 pips), and that's where you will be stopped. Very cool, no?

One-cancels-the-other orders

A *one-cancels-the-other order* (better known as the OCO order) is a stop-loss order associated with a profit order. An OCO claim is the definitive insurance policy for any open position. Your position remains open until one of the order levels is reached by the market and closes your position.

When one command level is reached and triggered, the other command is automatically canceled.

Say you have a short USD / JPY at 117.00. Do you think that if you go over 117.50, you will continue to increase, so that's where you wish to place your stop loss buy order? At the same time, you think the USD / JPY has a negative potential

116.25, this is where you set your purchase order cost-effectively. You now have two bracketing orders on the market, and your risk is clearly defined. As long as the market is trading between 116.26 and 117.49, its position will remain open. If 116.25 is reached first, your profit is triggered, and you redeem with profit. If 117.50 is reached first, your position will be interrupted.

OCO orders are strongly recommended for all open positions.

Contingent orders

A *contingent order* is a sophisticated term for combining different types of orders to create a comprehensive currency trading strategy. Use contingent orders to negotiate while you are asleep or sick, knowing that your contingent order has all the bases taken care of, and your risks are defined. Contingency commands are also called *if/then* commands. The if/then requests require that the request *if* one *makes* first and *then* the second part of the application becomes active; therefore, they are sometimes called *if done/then* requests .

The main feature of an order of most political brokers is that their orders are executed based on the *difference* in *prices* of the trading platform. This means that your limited purchase order is executed only if the offer price of the trading platform reaches your purchase rate. A sell limit order is triggered only if the bid price of the trading platform reaches its selling rate.

In practice, say you have a EUR / USD buy order at 1.2855, and the broker's EUR / USD spread is 3 pips. Your purchase order will only be filled if the price of the platform is 1.2852 / 55. If the least price is 1.2853 / 56, no cigar because the lowest offer of the broker of 56 has never reached its purchase rate of 55 The same goes for limited sales orders.

The stop loss execution policies are slightly different from those of stock trading.

Stop-loss orders for sale are triggered if the broker 's *bid* price reaches its stop-loss order rate. Specifically, if your stop-loss order is sold at 1.2820 and the broker's lowest price is 1.2820 / 23, your stop will get filled at 1.2820.

The stop-loss orders are triggered if the price of the *offer of* the platform reaches its stop-loss rate. If your stop order is at 1.2875 and the dealer's high rate is 1.2872 / 75, your stop will get filled at 1.2875.

The advantage of this practice is that some companies guarantee against the slippage of their stop-loss orders under normal commercial conditions. (Rarely, if ever, a broker will guarantee losses by publishing economic reports.) The disadvantage is that your order will likely be triggered earlier than orders with losses in other markets, so you'll need to add a little more cushion by placing them on your forex platform.

Managing the Trade

So, you pulled the trigger and the open position, and you are now on the market. It's time to relax and let the market do what's right, right? Not so fast, my friend. The forex market is not a roulette where you place your bets, watch the wheel spin, and simply get the results. It is a dynamic and fluid environment where new information and price developments create new opportunities and change previous expectations.

We hope you will deliberate on our recommendations to always negotiate with a plan - by identifying beforehand where to enter and where to exit all transactions based on stop loss and profit. Conclusion: You increase your overall chances of commercial success (and minimize the risks involved) by carefully planning each transaction before engaging with the emotions and noise of the market.

Depending on the trading style you are looking for (short term versus medium and long term) and general market conditions (range versus trend limit), you will have more or less to do when managing an open position. If you follow a medium and long-term strategy with generally broader stop-loss and profit-taking parameters, you may prefer to follow the established and forgotten business plan that you have developed. But many things can happen between the moment you open a transaction, and the prices reach one of your trading levels. Therefore, staying at the top of the market is always a good idea, even for long-term trading.

Monitor the market while your transaction is active

Whichever trading style you follow, it's worth keeping up with market news and price developments while your trading is active. Unexpected news affecting your position could hit the market at any time. The news is news; By definition, you could not have explained this in your trading plan, so new news may require changes in your trading plan.

When we are talking about carrying out changes on the market plan, we are simply referring to reducing the risk of global trading by making a profit (total or partial) or by moving the stop loss in the way of trading. The idea is to be dynamic and fluid in one way: to make a profit and to reduce risks. Keep your breakpoint where you decided to go before you enter the trade.

Stay tuned for news and data

If your business logic depends on certain data or event expectations, you should be particularly careful about future reports on these topics.

Part of its calculation of shortening the EUR / USD, for example, may be based on the idea that inflationary pressures in the euro area are retreating, suggesting a decline in interest rates in the euro area to come. If the ratio of the price index for consumption (CPI) for the euro area the next day confirms his view, the fundamental basis of maintaining the strategy will be strengthened. You can determine if you want to increase your profit target based on the market reaction. Similarly, if the CPI report comes out unexpectedly, the fundamental basis of its trade is seriously compromised and serves as a clue to exit trade earlier than expected.

Each trading strategy must take into account news and upcoming data events before opening the position. Ideally, you should be aware of any data reports and news events that must occur during the expected time horizon of your trading strategy. You must also have a good understanding of what the market expects in terms of event results to anticipate the likely market reaction.

Look at other financial markets

Forex markets operate alongside other major financial markets such as stocks, bonds, and commodities (e.g., gold, oil, etc.). There are important psychological and fundamental relationships (discussed in more detail in Chapter 1) between other markets and currencies, especially the US dollar, so look for developments in other financial markets to see if they confirm or contradict the price movements of the pairs of dollars.

Evaluate your trading results

Whatever the outcome of any negotiation, you want to review the whole process to understand what you have done right and wrong. In particular, ask yourself the following questions:

How did you identify the business opportunity? Was it based on fundamental analysis, a technical vision, or a combination of both? Looking at your business in this way helps you identify your strengths and weaknesses as a technical or fundamental trader. For instance, if technical analysis generates more of your winning trades, you will probably want to devote more energy to this approach.

How was your business plan? Was the size of the position sufficient to match the risk and reward scenarios, or was it too big or too small? Could you have reached a better level? What tools did you use to improve entry time? Have you been patient enough, or have you been quick to think that you have never had the opportunity again? Was your profit realistic or twisted in the sky? Has the market respected your choice of profit levels, or have prices reached this value? Ask the same questions about your stop loss level. Use the answers to refine the size of your position, entry-level, and order placement in the future.

How well did you carry out the trade after it opened? Have you been able to monitor the market while your transaction was active effectively? If yes, how? If not, why not? The solutions to these questions show volumes about the time and dedication you can devote to your trading. Have you changed your business plan along the way? Have you adjusted stop-loss orders to protect profits? Did you make a partial profit? Have you closed the deal based on your trading plan, or have you been surprised by the market? Based on your answers, you will learn what role your emotions can play and what a professional's discipline is.

There are no good and bad answers in this review process; be as honest with yourself as possible. No one else will know your answers, and you have everything to gain by identifying what you are good at, what is not so good, and how you, as a currency trader, should get closer to the market.

Currency trading is about getting what you put in it. Regularly evaluating your trading results is an essential step to improve your trading skills, refine your trading styles, maximize your trading strengths, and minimize your trading weaknesses.

Before getting involved in trading actively forex market, take a step back, and think about how you want to approach the market. There is much more to currency trading than it seems, and we believe that the trading style you pick is one of the most important determinants of the overall success of trading.

This chapter presents the main points to consider when defining your own approach to currency trading. We analyze the characteristics of some of the most commonly applied trading styles and discuss their concrete meaning. We also present the essential elements of developing and adhering to a business plan.

FINDING THE RIGHT TRADING STYLE FOR YOU

We are often questioned, "What is the best way to trade on the foreign exchange market?" This is a delicate question that seems to imply that there is a good and a bad way to trade currencies. Unfortunately, there is no easy answer. Better to say, there is no *model* answer - that applies to everyone.

The characteristics of forex trading have something to offer to all styles of trading (long term, medium-term, or short term) and the approach (technical, fundamental, or mixed). Therefore, in deciding the style or approach that best suits the currencies, the starting point is not the exchange market itself, but its individual situation and thinking.

REAL-WORLD AND LIFESTYLE CONSIDERATIONS

Before you begin to identify the style and approach to trading that's right for you, think carefully about the resources you have to support your trading. As in most of the efforts of life , when it comes to trading on the financial market, there are two main features that people seem never enough: time and money. Deciding how much each one you can spend on currency trading helps to establish how you are pursuing your trading goals.

If you are a full-time trader, you have a lot of time to devote to market analysis and trading in the market. But as currencies are traded nonstop, you must always know which trading session you are trading in and the daily peaks and valleys of activity and liquidity. (See Chapter 1 for specific session details.) Just because the market is always open does not mean it's always a perfect time to trade.

If you own a full-time job, your boss may not like to take the time to follow charts or economic data reports while you are at work. This implies that you will have to use your free time to do your market research. Be realistic in thinking about how much time you can regularly spend, taking into account family obligations and other personal circumstances.

As far as money is concerned, we can not emphasize enough that commercial capital must be venture capital, and you should never risk money that you can not afford to lose. The default definition of *venture capital* is money that, if lost, will not significantly affect your standard of living. Needless to say, borrowed money is not ventured capital - you should never use borrowed money for speculative transactions.

By determining the amount of venture capital you have for trading, you'll have a better idea of the size of the account you can trade and the size of the position you can manage. Most online trading platforms usually offer generous leverage ratios that let you control a larger position with less margin required. But it's not because they offer high leverage that you need to use it fully.

MAKING TIME FOR MARKET ANALYSIS

Calculating the amount of data and news that flows through the forex market on a daily basis can be really overwhelming. So, how can a trader track all the data and news?

The key is to develop an effective daily market analysis routine. Through the internet and online currency brokers, independent traders can access a variety of information.

TECHNICAL VERSUS FUNDAMENTAL ANALYSIS

Ask yourself on what basis will you make your business decisions - fundamental analysis or technical analysis?

The bottom line is the large pool of news and information that reflects the macroeconomic and political fortunes of countries whose currencies are traded. In most cases, when you hear someone talking about the fundamentals of a currency, it refers to economic fundamentals. Economic fundamentals are based on:

- Economic data reports
- Interest rate levels
- Monetary Policy
- International trade flows
- International investment flows

The *technical* term refers to *technical analysis,* a form of market analysis that typically involves graphical analysis, trend line analysis, and mathematical studies of price behavior, such as momentum or moving averages. to name a few.

We do not know many currency traders who do not follow any form of technical analysis in their trading. Even stereotypical marketers who practice anything are probably aware of the technical price levels identified by others. If you are a trader active in other financial markets, you have probably done a technical analysis or at least heard about it.

The followers of each discipline have always debated the approach that works best. Instead of taking sides, we suggest following an approach that combines the two disciplines. In our knowledge, macroeconomic factors such as relative growth rates, interest rates, and market sentiment determine the general direction of exchange rates. But currencies seldom move in a straight line, which means that there are many short-term price movements to take advantage of - and some of them may be important.

Technical analysis can provide insights into the path of major price changes, allowing traders to predict the scope and direction of future price changes more accurately. More importantly, technical analysis is the key to building a well-defined trading strategy. For instance, your fundamental analysis, data expectations, or simple instinct may lead you to conclude that the USD / JPY is down. But where exactly do you fail? Where do you make profits, and where do you reduce your losses? You can use technical analysis to refine the points of entry and exit of trading and decide if and where to add positions or reduce them.

Sometimes foreign markets seem to be more due to fundamental factors such as current economic data and comments from a central bank official. At that time, the foundations provide the catalysts for breaks and technical reversals. At other times, technical growth seems to be leading the charge - an interruption in trend line support can trigger long-term stop-loss sales and incorporate system models that are sold according to the interruption of support. Later economic reports may be against directional theft, but the data must be damaged - the media is finished, and the market is selling.

The market approach with a mix of fundamental and technical analysis increases your chances of detecting business opportunities and managing your business more effectively. You will also be better prepared to deal with markets that react alternatively to key technical developments or a combination of both.

DIFFERENT STROKES FOR DIFFERENT FOLKS

Once you have thought about the time and resources you can devote to currency trading and the approach you favor (technical, fundamental, or mixed), the next step is to choose the trading style that you want. is best. corresponds to these choices

There are as many trading styles and different market approaches to the foreign exchange market as there are individuals in the foreign exchange market. But most marketing styles can be grouped into three major categories that boil down to varying degrees of market risk exposure. The two major elements of trade risk are time and relative price movements. How much more you hold a position, the higher the risk is exposed. The more you anticipate a price change, the more you are exposed to risk.

In the following segments, we detail the three main trading styles and what they really mean for individual traders. Our goal here is not to advocate a particular trading style because styles often overlap, and you can adopt different styles for different business opportunities or different market conditions. Instead, our goal is to give an idea of the different approaches used by forex traders so that you can fully understand the basis of each style.

SHORT-TERM, HIGH-FREQUENCY DAY TRADING

Short-term currency trading is different from short-term trading in most other markets. Short-Term trading of stocks or commodities usually means holding a position for one day for at least several days. However, due to liquidity and low spreads of supply and supply in currencies, prices fluctuate constantly in small increments. Constant and fluid currency price action allows speculators to trade on a very short-term basis and only want to capture a few pips (explained in Chapter 2) in each transaction.

Short-term forex trading usually involves maintaining a position for a few seconds or minutes and rarely more than an hour. But the time factor is not the defining quality of short-term currency trading. Instead, pip fluctuations are important. Traders who follow a short-term trading style seek to profit by opening and closing positions multiple times after winning only a few pips, often as little as 1 or 2 pips.

In the interbank market, very short-term incoming and outgoing exchanges are called *jobbing the market*; Online currency traders call it *scalping*. (We use terms interchangeably.) Traders who follow this style should be among the fastest and most disciplined traders because they only want to capture a few pips in each trade. In terms of speed, quick response and instant decision-making are essential to succeed in the job market.

When it comes to discipline, stockbrokers must be absolutely cruel when they make profits and losses. If you only wish to make a few pips in each trade, you can not lose much more than a few pips in each trade.

Working on the market requires an intuitive understanding of the market. (Some practitioners call this *rhythm trading.*) Money changers do not care much about fundamentals. If you ask a scalper for his opinion on a specific currency pair, she is likely to respond to the "Looks *Bid* " or "Looks *Offered* " lines (that is, she feels buying or underlying sales in the market - but at that time). If you ask again a few minutes later, she can answer in the opposite direction.

Successful stockbrokers have absolutely no loyalty to one position. They would not care less if the currency pair went up or down. They are strictly focused on next glitches. Their position works for them, or they come out faster than you can blink. All they need is volatility and liquidity.

Retail traders are generally faced with discrepancies between offers and offers between 2 and 5 pips. While this makes the job a bit more difficult, it does not mean that you can not still engage in short-term negotiations - it simply means that you will need to adjust the risk parameters of the style. Instead of trying to make 1 to 2 pips in each transaction, you need to get a pip gain at least as big as the spread with which you trade in each currency pair. The other basic rules of only minimal losses and not staying in the same position for a long time still apply.

Here are some other essential guidelines to bear in mind when following a short-term trading strategy:

- **Only trade in the most liquid currency pairs such as EUR / USD, USD / JPY, EUR / GBP, EUR / JPY, and**

EUR / CHF. The most liquid pairs have the narrowest trading spreads and the least sudden price jumps.

• **Only trade during peak periods of liquidity and market interest.** Constant liquidity and smooth market interest are essential for short-term trading strategies. Market liquidity is deeper in the course of the European session when the centers business in Asia and America north to overshadow European areas of time - about two in the morning to noon (the Eastern States - the US). Trading in other sessions may leave you with less predictable short-term price movements that you can take advantage of.

• **Concentrate your trading on one pair at a time.** If you plan to capture price movements from second to second or minute to minute, you need to focus fully on one pair at a time. This will also improve your perception of the pair if this pair is everything you look at.

• **You have predefined your default trading size, so you do not have to specify it in each transaction.**

• **Find a brokerage firm that offers clicks and transactions, so you do not experience delays or foreclosures.**

• **Modify your risk and reward expectations to reflect the trading spread of the currency pair you are trading.** With spreads of 2 to 5 pip on most major pairs, you will likely need to capture 3 to 10 pip per transaction to make up for losses if the market moves against you.

- **Avoid trading around dice throwing.** Taking a short-term position in a data publication is very risky because prices can skyrocket after launch, throwing a short-term strategy out of the water. Markets are also subject to rapid price adjustments between 15 and 30 minutes prior to the release of key data when closing orders are triggered. This can result in a rapid change of position, which may not be resolved before the data is released.

MEDIUM-TERM DIRECTIONAL TRADING

Medium-term positions are generally busy for periods ranging from minutes to hours, but usually not much more than a day. As with short-term trading, the main distinction of medium-term trading is not the opening time of the position, but the number of pips you seek / risk.

When short-term traders seek to take advantage of the routine noise of small price movements, almost disregarding the general direction of the market, medium-term transactions seek to gain the right direction and benefit from more favorable exchange rate movements. important.

Almost as many currency investors fall into the medium-term category (sometimes called *momentum trading* and *swing trading*) as in the short-term category. Medium-term trading needs many of the same skills as short-term trading, particularly with respect to entry / exit positions, but it also requires a broader perspective, a greater analysis effort, and a lot more patience.

Capturing intraday price movements for maximum effect

The benefit of medium-term trading is to determine where a currency pair is likely to move in the next hours or days and developing a trading strategy to exploit that vision. Medium-term traders usually follow one of the following general approaches, with plenty of room to combine strategies:

- **Trading a View:** Have a basic opinion about how a currency pair will likely evolve. The display operations are generally based on prevailing market themes, such as interest rate expectations or economic growth trends. Display traders must always be aware of technical levels as part of a global trading plan.
- **Trading the technical:** Base your market perspective on graphical models, trend lines, support and resistance levels, and momentum studies. Technical traders usually identify a trading opportunity in their charts, but they must always be aware of key events because they are the catalyst for many technical breaks.
- **Trading Events and Data:** Base your positions on the results of expected events, such as a rate decision from the central bank or a G7 meeting or individual data reports. Event / data traders usually open positions well in advance and close them when the result is known.
- **Trading with the flow:** Trading based on the general direction of the market (trend) or on the main purchases and sales (flows). To trade with feed information, look for a broker that offers feedback on

the market flow, such as the one found
on FOREX.com *Forex
Insider* (www.forex.com/forex_research.html). Flow
traders tend to be excluded from limited markets at
short-term intervals and only enter when market
movement is underway.

WHEN IS A TREND NOT A TREND?

When it's a trading range, a *range* or *market-related to* a *range* is
a market that remains confined to a relatively narrow price
range. In currency pairs, a short-term trading range (in the
next few hours) may have a width of 20 to 50 pips, while a
long-term trading range (in the next few days or weeks) may
have a range of 20 to 50 pips. width from 200 to 400
pips.

Despite all the hype that trends have in various market
publications, the reality is that most markets do not tend to be
over a third of the time. The rest of the time, they jump at
intervals, consolidate, and exchange laterally.

While mid-term traders seek to capture larger relative price
movements - say, 50 to 100 pips or more - they also quickly
realize smaller profits on the basis of short-term price
behavior. For example, if a violation of a technical resistance
level suggests a higher target price move of 80 pips toward the
next resistance level, the medium-term trader will be more
than happy to capture 70% to 80% of the next resistance level.
Expected price movement. They will not stay in position in
search of the exact price to reach.

LONG-TERM MACROECONOMIC TRADING

Long-term currency trading is generally reserved for hedge funds and other institutional types. Long-term currency trading may involve holding positions for weeks, months, and potentially years at a time. Holding positions over this period necessarily involves being exposed to significant short-term volatility that can quickly overwhelm margin trading accounts.

With appropriate risk management, individual margin traders can seek to capture long-term trends. The key is to maintain a small enough position relative to your margin balance to withstand the volatility of up to 5% or more.

CARRY TRADE STRATEGIES

A *carry trade* occurs when you buy a high yielding currency and sell a lower-yielding currency. The strategy profits in two ways:

> **• Being long the highest yielding currency and short the lowest yielding currency, you can get the interest rate differential between the two currencies, called** *carry.* If you have the opposite position - buy the smallest and the smallest - the interest rate differential is against you and is known as the *cost of shipping.*
> **• Spot prices rise in the direction of the interest rate differential.** Currency pairs with large interest rate

differentials tend to move in favor of the higher-yielding currency as long traders are rewarded, increasing buying interests, and short traders are penalized, reducing the interest of sale.

So, let me clarify: you may be thinking: all I have to do is buy the most profitable currency / sell the worst-performing currency, sit down, earn the carry, and to watch the spot price rise? What is the question?

The problem is that the negative volatility of spot prices can quickly erase any gain in the carry trade differential. The risk can be exacerbated by the over-positioning of the market in favor of the carry trade, which means that they carry trade has become so popular that everyone gets into it.

Carry trades generally work best in low volatility environments, for example, when the financial markets are relatively steady, and investors are forced to chase yield. Remember that carry trades need to have a significant differential in interest rates between the two currencies (usually over 2%) to make them attractive. And carry trade is certainly a long-term strategy because depending on when you enter, you can be caught in a downdraft that can take days or weeks to relax before the trade becomes profitable again.

DEVELOPING A DISCIPLINED TRADING PLAN

Whatever trading style you decide to adopt, you need an organized trading plan, or it does not go very far. The difference between losing cash and making cash in the foreign exchange market can be as simple as trading without a plan or trading with it. A *trading plan* is a prepared approach to execute a trading strategy that you have developed based on your analysis and market outlook.

Here are the main elements of any business plan:

- **Determine the size of the position:** what is the size of your position for each trading strategy? The size of the position is half the equation to determine how much money is involved in each transaction.
- **Decide where to get into the position:** where exactly are you going to try to open the desired position? What happens if your entry-level is not reached?
- **Setting Stop Loss and Take Profit Levels:** Where exactly will you leave the position if it is a winning position (make a profit) and if it is a stop position? The stop-loss and take-profit levels are the second half of the equation that determines how much money is involved in each transaction.

That's it - just three simple components. But it's amazing how many new and seasoned traders open positions without ever thinking fully about their game plan. Of course, there are several tricky points to consider when developing a trading plan. But for the moment, we just want to get back to the point where negotiating without an organized plan is like flying a plane blindfolded - you can take off, but how are you going to land?

And regardless of how good your trading plan is, it will not work if you do not follow it. Sometimes, emotions arise and distract traders from their trading plans. Other times, unexpected news or a price movement forces traders to abandon their trading strategy halfway, or in the middle of trading , as the case may be. Anyway, when that happens, it's the same as never having a business plan in the first place.

Developing a market plan and sticking to it are the two main ingredients of *corporate discipline.* If we name the trait that defines successful traders, it would not be technical analysis skills, instinct, or aggression - although they are all important. No, it would be a commercial discipline. Traders who follow a disciplined approach are those who survive year after year and cycle aftermarket. They can even make mistakes more often and continue to make money because they follow a disciplined approach.

TAKING THE EMOTION OUT OF TRADING

If the key to fruitful trading is a disciplined tactic - developing a trading plan and making use of it - why is it so difficult for many traders to practice trading discipline? The answer is complex, but it usually comes down to a simple case of human emotions that takes them away. Do not underestimate the power of emotions to distract and disturb.

So, how do you get the thrill of trading? The answer is simple: you can not. As far as your heart beats and your synapses fly away, the emotions will flow. And, to be honest, the high emotional levels of business are one of the reasons people get attracted to it in the first place. There is no hurry to doing business successfully and withdrawing money from the market. So accept that you will experience quite intense emotions during the negotiation.

The long answer is that because you can not block emotions, the best you hope to achieve is to understand where the emotions come from, recognize them when they hit, and limit the impact on your negotiations. It's very easy to say, but bear in mind some of the following to keep your emotions under control:

- **Concentrate on pips, not on dollars and cents.** Do not be distracted by the exact amount of money earned or lost in the exchange. Instead, focus on where the prices are and how they behave. The market has no idea how big your business is and how much you win or lose, but you know where the present price is.
- **It's not about being wrong or right; It's about making money.** The market does not care whether you are right or wrong, and you should not either. The only real method used to measure a company's success is in dollars and cents.
- **You will lose in a reasonable number of transactions.** No operator is always right. Taking losses

is as routine as making profits. You can always succeed over time with a solid risk management plan.

Technical and fundamental analysis are the two major areas of the FOREX market strategy, which is exactly the same as in the stock market. However, technical analysis is the most common strategy used by individual FOREX traders. Here is a brief summary of both forms of analysis and how they apply directly to forex trading:

FUNDAMENTAL ANALYSIS

If you have trouble evaluating a company, try to evaluate an entire country. Fundamental analysis of the foreign exchange market is often extremely difficult and is generally only used as a means of predicting long-term trends. However, it is essential to mention that some traders negotiate strictly in the short term in press releases. There are many different fundamental indicators of monetary values published at many different times. Here are some to help you get started:

- Non-agricultural payroll
- Purchasing Managers Index (PMI)
- Consumer Price Index (CPI)
- Retail sales
- Durable goods

You should know that these reports are not the only fundamental factors to note. There are also a variety of meetings where you can get quotes and comments that can affect the markets as much as any report. These meetings are often held to discuss interest rates, inflation, and other issues that may affect the value of currencies.

Even changes in the way things are formulated to solve certain problems, such as the comments of the Chairman of the Federal Reserve on interest rates, can cause a volatile market. Two vital meetings to note are the Federal Open Market Committee and the Humphrey Hawkins Hearings.

By reading the reports and reviewing the comments, you can help FOREX's fundamental analysts better understand all the long-term market trends and also allow short-term traders to take advantage of extraordinary events. If you decide to follow a key strategy, always keep an economic calendar at hand to know when these reports will be published. Your broker may also provide you with real-time access to this type of information.

TECHNICAL ANALYSIS

Like their counterparts in the stock markets, FOREX technical analysts analyze price trends. The only major difference between technical analysis in FOREX and technical analysis in stocks is the period involved in the 24-hour FOREX markets.

For this reason, some time-sensitive forms of technical analysis need to be modified to work with the 24-hour FOREX market. Some of the major forms of technical analysis used in FOREX are:

- Elliott's waves
- Fibonacci studies
- Parabolic SAR
- Pivot points

Many technical analysts tend to combine technical studies to make more accurate predictions on their behalf. (The most common technique for them is merging the Fibonacci studies with Elliott Waves.) Others prefer to set up the systems negotiation in order to locate repeatedly conditions of purchase and sale of similar. Using a profitable trading system with a demo account for a few weeks is a great way to get an accurate "feel" of Forex trading - without risking your own money!

BEST FOREX TRADING STRATEGIES THAT WORK

You may have been told that maintaining your discipline is an essential aspect of trading. While this is true, how can you make sure that you apply this discipline during a negotiation? One way to help is to possess a trading strategy that you can follow. If it is well-founded and retested, you can be sure that you are using one of the successful Forex trading strategies. This trust will allow you to follow the rules of your strategy more easily - so maintain your discipline.

Often, when people talk about Forex strategies, they talk about a specific trading technique that is usually just one facet of a whole trading plan. A consistent Forex trading strategy gives beneficial input signals, but it is also essential to consider:

- Position sizing
- Risk management
- How to exit a trade

CHOOSING THE BEST FOREX AND CFD STRATEGY FOR YOU IN 2021

When it comes to clarifying what the most profitable and best forex trading strategy is, there is really no single answer. Here's why. The best exchange strategies will be adapted to the individual. This means that you have to consider your personality and find the best Forex strategy for you. What can work for someone else can be a disaster for you.

On the other hand, a strategy that has been ignored by others may be right for you. Therefore, it may be necessary to experiment to discover the Forex trading strategies that work. Conversely, it can remove those that do not work for you. One of the major factors to consider is a delay in your trading style.

There are different types of trading styles (as discussed in the previous chapter), short-term, and these have been widely used in previous years and still remain a popular option on the list of best trading strategies Forex on the market. 2021. The best forex traders are always aware of the different styles and strategies in their quest to know how to trade forex successfully so they can pick the right one based on current market conditions.

50-Pips a Day Forex Strategy

This strategy is based on the initial market movements of certain highly liquid currency pairs. The GBPUSD and EURUSD currency pairs are among the best currencies to trade using this particular strategy. After the candlestick closes at 7:00 GMT, traders place two opposing positions or two orders on hold. When one of them is activated by the price movements, the other position is automatically canceled.

The profit target is placed at 50 pips, while the stop-loss order is placed between 5 and 10 pips above or below the candlestick at 7:00 GMT after its formation. This is implemented to manage the risks. Once these conditions are set, it is now up to the market to take over. Day trading and scalping are short-term trading strategies. However, keep in mind that shorter time frames imply a higher risk; Therefore, effective risk management is essential.

Forex Daily Charts Strategy

The best forex traders swear on daily charts of shorter-term strategies. Compared to the one-hour forex trading strategy or even shorter deadlines, there is less market noise involved in daily charts. These charts can provide more than 100 pips a day because of their long run, which can result in some of the best forex deals.

Trading signals are more reliable, and the profit potential is much higher. The trader also doesn't need to worry about daily needs and random price fluctuations. The method is based on three main principles:

- Spot the trend: Markets tend to consolidate, and this process is repeated in cycles. The first feature of this style is to find prolonged movements in the currency markets. One way to identify forex trends is to study 180 periods in forex data. Identifying the ups and downs of the balance sheet will be the next step. By referencing these price data on the current charts, you can identify the direction of the market.
- Stay focused: it requires patience, and you will have to get rid of the desire to enter the market immediately. You must stay away and preserve your capital for a greater opportunity.
- Less leverage and more downtime: be aware of the large intraday market fluctuations. However, using larger stops does not mean endangering large amounts of capital.

Although there are many trading strategies guides available for professional forex traders, the best Forex strategy for consistent earnings can only be obtained through in-depth practice. Here are some other strategies you can try:

Forex 1-Hour Trading Strategy

You can take advantage of the 60-minute delay in this strategy. The greatest currency pairs to trade using this strategy are EUR / USD, USD / JPY, GBP / USD, and AUD / USD. You would need a 100pip moment indicator and indicator arrows, both available in MetaTrader 4.

Rules of buy trade:

You can enter a long position once both conditions are met:

- The Momentum 100 pips indicator triggers a buy signal when its blue line crosses the red line below
- The indicator arrow emits a green arrow signal

In this case, you can place the stop loss under the red indicator line or the most recent support line. You can close trading after 30 pips or make a profit when the indicator arrows emit a red arrow signal.

Rules of Sell Trade:

You may enter a short position once the following conditions are true:

- The Momentum 100 pips indicator triggers a sell signal when its blue line crosses the red line above
- Indicator arrows emit a red arrow signal

Place the stop loss above the red indicator line or the most recent resistance line. Close trading after 30 points, or when the indicator arrows give a green arrow signal.

Forex weekly trading strategy

While many forex traders prefer intraday trading, as market volatility offers more profit opportunities in the shorter term, weekly forex trading strategies can offer more flexibility and stability. A weekly candlestick provides complete information on the market. It contains five daily candles and changes that reflect the actual market trends. The weekly forex trading strategies are based on lower position sizes and avoid excessive risk.

For this strategy, we will make use of the exponential moving average (EMA) indicator. The last daily candlestick of the previous week should close at a level above the EMA value. Now, we have to search for the moment when the high level of the previous week was broken. Then a buy stop order is placed in the H4 closed candlestick at the broken level price level.

The stop loss should be put at the nearest minimum point, between 50 and 105 pips. The previous extreme value is used for calculations if the nearest minimum point is closer to 50 pips. Here, last week's range of motion is considered the profit range.

The role of stock price trading in Forex strategies

The extent to which fundamentals are used varies from trader to trader. At the same time, the best strategy invariably utilizes action. This also is known as technical analysis. As far as technical currency trading strategies are concerned, there are two main styles: tracking trends and counter-trend trading. Both currency trading strategies attempt to profit by recognizing and exploiting price models.

In terms of price models, the most important concepts include concepts such as support and resistance. In simple terms, these terms represent a market's tendency to recover from previous highs and lows. Support is the market trend to increase from a previously established minimum level. Resistance is the ability of the market to fall from a previously established high. Indeed, market players tend to judge subsequent prices against recent lows and highs.

What transpires when the market is approaching recent lows? In other words, buyers will be attracted by what they consider cheap. What happens when the trade approaches recent highs? Sellers will be attracted by what they consider to be expensive or a good place to make a profit. As a result, recent ups and downs are the criteria by which current prices are valued.

There is also a self-fulfilling aspect of the support and resistance levels. Indeed, market players anticipate some price action at these points and act accordingly. Therefore, their actions can contribute to market behavior as expected.

However, these three things should be noted:

- Support and resistance levels do not have strict rules; they are simply a common consequence of the natural behavior of market players.
- Trend tracking systems aim to take advantage of times when levels of support and resistance are deteriorating.
- Counter-trend trading styles are the opposite of trend tracking - they are meant to sell when there is a new higher and buy when there is a new low.

Trend-Following Forex Strategies

Sometimes a market comes out of the beach, moving under the rack or over the resistance to start a trend. How does this happen? As support breaks and the market moves to new lows, buyers begin to postpone. In fact, buyers constantly realize lower prices and want to wait for a fund to be reached. Similarly, there will be traders who sell in panic or are simply forced to leave their positions.

The trend remains until the end of the sale, and the belief begins to return to buyers when it is determined that prices will no longer fall. Trend tracking strategies encourage traders to buy in the markets after breaking resistance and selling markets, and when they fall into support levels.

In addition, trends can also be dramatic and prolonged. Due to the magnitude of the movements involved, this type of system has the potential to be the most successful Forex trading strategy. Trend tracking systems use indicators to inform traders when a new trend may have started, but there is no sure way to know, of course.

Here is the good news:

If the indicator can set a time when it is more likely that a trend has started, you are tipping the odds in your favor. The indication that a trend can form is called a leak. An interruption occurs when the price exceeds the highest or lowest maximum for a specified number of days. For example, a 20-day break occurs when the price exceeds the highest peak of the last 20 days.

Trend monitoring systems require a specific state of mind because of the long duration - during which the benefits may disappear as the market swings - these trades may be more psychologically demanding. When markets are volatile, trends tend to be more disguised, and price fluctuations are greater. Therefore, a trend tracking system is the best trading strategy for Forex markets that are calm and trendy.

A good example of a simple trend tracking strategy is the Donchian Trend system. The Donchian channels were invented by futures trader Richard Donchian and are trend indicators in the process of being established. The Donchian channel's parameter can be altered as you see fit, but in this example, we will see a leak of 20 days.

Basically, Donchian channel breakout suggests two things:

- Buy if the market price exceeds the highest of the last 20 days
- Sell if the price falls below the 20-day low.

There is an additional rule for trade when the market condition is more favorable to the system. This rule is designed to filter leaks that go against the long-term trend. In summary, you analyze the 25-day moving average (MA) and the 300-day moving average. The direction of the shortest moving average determines the allowed direction. This rule allows you only to go:

- Short if the 25-day moving average is below the 300-day moving average

OR

- Long if the 25-day moving average is above the 300-day moving average
- The negotiations end similarly to the entry but only with a 10-day break. This implies that if you open a long position and the market falls below the previous 10-day low, you can sell to exit the trade - and vice versa.

4-Hour Forex Trading Strategy

A potentially beneficial and profitable Forex trading strategy is the 4-hour trend strategy. However, the four-hour delay makes it more appropriate for swing traders. This strategy makes use of a 4-hour base chart to track the potential locations of trading signals. The one-hour graph is used as a signal graph to determine where the actual positions will be taken.

Always remember that the time period for the signal graph must be at least one hour shorter than the basic graph. Two sets of MA lines will be selected. One will be the MA of 34 periods, while the other will be the MA of 55 periods. To see if a trend is worth exchanging, MA lines will have to be linked to price action.

In the case of an uptrend, the conditions that will be fulfilled are as follows:

- The price will remain higher than the MA lines
- Line 34-MA will remain above line 55-MA and continue to do so.
- MA lines tilt-up for the maximum duration during an uptrend
- In the case of a downtrend, the following conditions will be met:
- Price action will remain below two MA lines
- Line 34-MA will remain below line 55-MA and continue to do so.
- MA lines go down for a maximum duration

The MA lines will become a support zone during bullish trends, and there will be resistance zones during downtrends. It is in and around this area that the best positions for the trend strategy can be found. Learn how to negotiate step by step with our new educational course, Forex 101, with important information from industry experts.

Counter-Trend Forex Strategies

Counter-trend forex strategies are based on the fact that most leaks do not turn into long-term trends. Therefore, a trader using this strategy seeks to take advantage of the price trend to reflect the previously established-ups and downs. On paper, counter-trend forex strategies are the best Forex trading strategies to boost confidence because they have a high success rate.

However, it is essential to note that tight reins are needed on the risk management side. These Forex trading strategies are accompanied by levels of support and resistance. But there is also a risk of major disadvantages when these levels deteriorate. Continuous monitoring of the market is a good idea. The state of the market that best fits this type of strategy is stable and volatile. This type of environment provides market oscillations healthy pre ç is ã the limit in a range. It is important to note that the market may change state.

For example, a stable and calm market can start the trend, remain stable, become volatile as the trend develops. How the state of a market can change is uncertain. You need to look for evidence of the current state to find out if it fits your trading style.

88

CHOOSING YOUR STRATEGY

The most successful traders will develop a strategy and refine it for a specific period of time. Some people will focus on a specific study or calculation, while others will use a broad-based analysis to determine their business. Most experts probably suggest that you try to use a combination of fundamental and technical analysis, with which you can make long-term projections as well as determine the entry and exit points. Obviously, in the end, it is the professional who must decide what suits him best.

When you're ready to go into the FOREX market, open a demo account and paper exchange so you can practice until you make a steady profit . Many people who fail tend to enter the FOREX market and quickly lose a lot of money for lack of experience. It's important to take your time and learn how to trade properly before you start hiring capital.

You must also be able to exchange without emotion. You can not track all stop-loss points if you do not have the option to run them on time. You must always set your breakpoints and profit-taking points so that they automatically run and change them only when absolutely necessary. Make your decisions and stick to them. Otherwise, you will become crazy (and your brokers).

You must also realize that you must follow the trends. If you are against the trend, you are just playing with your money because the FOREX market tends to evolve more often than anything else, and you are more likely to succeed in trading with the trend.

The foreign exchange market is the largest market in the world, and every day people are more interested in it. But before you begin to trade, make sure your broker meets certain criteria and take the time to find a trading strategy that's right for you.

Learning to choose the right trading strategy for you can be difficult for beginners. Most Forex traders want to become rich in a short time from the time they start trading, but this is sometimes unrealistic.

You should also consider high-risk, high-return strategies versus low-risk, low-return strategies during the selection process to get the best trading strategy. Another important factor to consider is to test your strategy on a demo account.

Below you will find a list of Forex beginners strategy trading tips that will help you throughout your journey.

Select a strategy and stick to it.

This is very crucial for beginners. Avoid trading strategies all the time because it generates less profit. This is the tip that forex savvy traders use to make higher profits. They select a trading strategy and adhere to their specific strategy. So why do not you learn the hacks of experienced Forex traders and do not stick to your specific strategy?

Choose your broker wisely

This is another tip that can help you. Make sure to check the reviews and recommendations for choosing a reliable broker that fits your trading personality well. Remember that choosing the right broker is half the hassle. For your information, expect to find fake brokers who will stand in your way but choose an authorized broker with a license. You can do this by setting strict standards to be met by the broker you choose to protect your money.

Do not let your emotions take over.

You must always take control of your emotions, even if it is not easy, especially after suffering a series of defeats. If you let your emotions take you away, you expose yourself. Make sure you eliminate emotions, especially after deciding on your specific trading strategy. Traders who earn higher profits are generally calm all the time, whether the market is volatile or not. It allows them to make good decisions.

Make your own strategy.

The most common errors made by novice traders do not create their own action plans. You must know what you expect from trading. Make sure you have a well-thought-out end goal in mind to succeed in your trading discipline. In fact, it is suggested to use a Forex trading strategy consistent with your goals in order to quickly build your success.

Always practice.

They say that practice leads to perfection, and this is one of the crucial tips and tricks for novice traders. By practicing constantly, you increase the chances of consistently higher results. You may not want to lose money learning the basics, but the good thing is that testing your strategy on a demo account does not cost you anything to set up. Therefore, you must begin to learn the basics and slowly graduate until you understand the rules of the game.

Refrain from stressing yourself.

This is one of the Foreign exchange hacks, which is obvious. You must discover the source of your stress and try to eliminate it or minimize its influence on you. Breathing deeply and focusing on something else can be beneficial at this stage. You can use different ways to overcome stress, such as listening to music or exercising.

Currency trading can be devastating, especially for new traders who have no idea of the rules involved. There are different types of Forex trading strategies that you can decide to adopt. If you want to venture into Forex trading, there are many strategies to choose from. You must know what suits you.

However, you should know the advantages and disadvantages of each strategy, as well as the risks involved in each strategy.

This will help you evaluate the performance of the strategy of your choice. Most professional traders choose the trading day because it presents less risk of events that may have an impact on the share price aftermarket hours.

Conclusion

By following these hacks, during the process of choosing your Forex trading strategy, you need to know that without risk, there is no success. Therefore, when you choose to become a Forex trader, you must have already accepted the probability of failure.

WHAT IS A FOREX BROKER?

The brokers Forex are companies that provide specialist marketing with access to a flat - form that allows them to trade foreign currencies. Transactions on this market are always between a pair of two different currencies, so currency traders buy or sell the specific pair they wish to trade.

Forex brokers can also be called retail forex brokers or currency brokers. Most forex brokers only manage a very small portion of the overall volume of the foreign exchange market. Retail currency traders use these brokers to access the 24-hour currency market for speculative purposes. Forex brokerage services are also provided to institutional clients by large companies such as investment banks.

Main conclusions:

- Forex brokers allow traders to access the foreign exchange market.
- Most brokers serve retail clients, although large banking companies also serve institutional clients.
- Forex brokers let clients trade with very high leverage.
- Forex brokers make money primarily on buy and sell spreads, but may also have other ways to do so.

UNDERSTANDING THE ROLE OF A FOREX BROKER

Forex brokers give access to trading in all major currency pairs; EUR / USD, GBP / USD, USD / JPY, and USD / CHF, as well as other G10 currencies and all exchange rates between them. In addition, most brokers will allow clients to trade emerging market currencies.

A forex broker allows a trader to open a transaction by buying a currency pair and closing the deal by selling the same pair. For instance, if traders want to exchange euros for US dollars, they buy the EUR / USD pair. This is equivalent to buying euros in US dollars for the purchase. When they close the deal, they sell the pair, which is equivalent to buying US dollars and using euros to buy. If exchange rates were higher when traders closed, they would maintain profits. Otherwise, traders would notice a loss.

Forex brokers have improved their customer service over the years. Opening a forex trading account is usually quite simple and can be done online. Before trading, a forex broker will ask clients to deposit money into their accounts as collateral. However, the brokerage firm also provides its customers with effect from leverage so they can negotiate larger amounts than is deposited into their account. Depending on the trading country of the trader, this leverage can be 30 to 400 times the amount available on the trading account. High leverage makes forex trading very risky, and most traders lose money trying to trade this way.

HOW FOREX BROKERS MAKE MONEY

Forex brokers are compensated in two ways; First, through it's spread of buying and selling a currency pair. For example, when the euro-dollar pair is quoted at 1.120010 and 1.120022 ask, the difference between these two prices is 0.00012 or 1.2 pips. When a retail customer opens a position at the selling price and then closes the position in the offer price, the forex broker will have collected this spread value. Second, brokers may charge additional fees. Some may charge transaction fees or monthly fees for accessing a specific software interface, or fees for access to special commercial products such as exotic options. However, the competition between forex brokers is very intense, and most companies serving retail customers think they should attract customers by eliminating as many fees as possible. This has led many people to propose free or very low transaction costs beyond the spread.

Some forex brokers also earn money through their own trading operations. This can be problematic if your negotiations create a conflict of interest with your clients, but regulation in this area has helped to reduce this practice significantly.

REGULATION BETWEEN FOREX BROKERS

Two entities exercise regulatory functions between forex brokers to discourage and eliminate fraudulent practices: The National Futures Association and CFTC (Commodity Futures Trading Commission). These organizations pursue lawsuits against which their practices are considered fraudulent or intentionally prejudicial to their clients.

It is important to research whether a broker has an excellent reputation and the functionality you are looking for at a broker. This search can be done by visiting the NFA home page and reviewing the opinions of Investopedia brokers.

Most major forex brokers will allow potential customers to use a convenient account to understand better what the system looks like. It's a great idea to test as many platforms as possible before deciding which broker to use.

In addition, as the foreign exchange market is open 24 hours a day, most quality forex brokers will provide 24-hour service.

6 CRUCIAL THINGS TO TAKE INTO ACCOUNT TO CHOOSE A FOREX BROKER

The retail foreign exchange market is so competitive that just having to look at all the available brokers can cause a big headache.

Choosing the forex broker to trade can be a very overwhelming task, especially if you do not know what to look for.

In this part, we will discuss the features you should look for when choosing a forex broker.

1. Security

The first and foremost feature that a good broker should have is a high level of security. After all, you will not hand over thousands of dollars to someone who simply claims to be legitimate, right?

Fortunately, checking out the credibility of a forex broker is not very difficult. There are regulatory agencies around the world that separate fraudulent trust.

Here is a list of countries with their corresponding regulatory bodies:

- United Kingdom: Prudential Regulation Authority (PRA) and Financial Conduct Authority (FCA)
- United States of America: Commodity Futures Trading Commission (CFTC) and National Futures Association (NFA)
- Australia: Australian Securities and Investments Commission (ASIC)
- Germany: Bundesanstalt für Finanzdienstleistungsaufsicht (BaFin)
- Switzerland: Swiss Federal Banking Commission (SFBC)
- France: Autorité des Marchés Financiers (AMF)
- Before you even consider putting your money in a broker, make sure he is a member of the regulatory bodies mentioned above.

- Canada: Investment Information Regulatory Organization of Canada (IIROC)

2. Transaction costs

No matter what type of trader you are, whether you like it or not, you will still be subject to transaction fees.

Whenever you enter a trade, you will have to pay the spread or commission, so it is natural to look for the cheapest and cheapest rates.

Sometimes, you may have to sacrifice small transactions for a more reliable broker.

Make sure you need tight spreads for your type of trading and review the available options. It's about discovering the right balance between security and low transaction costs.

3. Deposit and withdrawal

Good currency brokers allow you to deposit funds and withdraw your winnings without complications.

Brokers have really no reason to make it difficult to withdraw their profits because the only reason they keep their funds is to facilitate transactions.

Your broker only holds your money to facilitate transactions, so there is no reason for you to have trouble getting the profits you have made. Your broker must ensure that the withdrawal process is fast and smooth.

4. Trading platform

In online forex trading, most trading activities are done through the broker's trading platform. This means that your broker's trading platform must be user-friendly and stable.

When searching for a broker, always look for what their trading platform has to offer.

Offer a free news feed? How about easy-to-use technical and graphical tools? Provides all the information you need to trade correctly?

5. Execution

Your broker must inform you at the best possible price for your orders.

Under normal market conditions (for instance, normal liquidity , no surprise events, or major press releases), there is no reason for your broker not to inform you of the market price you see when you pick on the "Buy" button or the button. "sell."

For instance, assuming you have a steady internet connection, if you click "buy" EUR / USD for 1.3000, it should be filled at this price or inside micro-pips. The speed at which your orders are executed is very important, especially if you change money.

A difference of a few pips in the price can make it very difficult to win this offer.

6. Customer service

Brokers are not perfect, so you must choose a broker that you can easily contact in case of problems.

Brokers' competence when dealing with the account or technical support issues is as important as their performance in executing trades.

Brokers can be helpful and kind during the account opening process, but they enjoy terrific after-sales support.

BROKERS YOU MUST AVOID

Just as there are brokers you want, there are also brokers you want to avoid. For example, brokers who are likely to buy or prematurely sell near predefined points (usually called sniping and hunting) are insignificant things that are done by brokers who are simply trying to increase their profits.

Obviously, no broker would agree to do this, but there are ways to know if a broker has committed this crime.

Unfortunately, the only way to really determine which brokers are doing this and which ones are not talking to other traders. There is no actual list or organization reporting this type of activity. The major point here is that you have to visit online discussion forums or talk to others in person to find out who is an honest broker.

Strict margin rules

When negotiating with borrowed money, your broker should have an opinion on the level of risk you can take. With this in mind, your broker can purchase or sell at your discretion, which can be a very bad thing for you.

Let's assume you own a margin account, and your position drops sharply before you start recovering at unprecedented highs. Even if you have enough money to cover it, some brokers will settle your position on a margin call at this low. This action on their part can be expensive. You talk to other people in person or visit online discussion forums to find out who the honest brokers are.

Registering for a FOREX account is very similar to obtaining a balance sheet account. The only big difference is that for FOREX accounts, you have to sign a margin contract.

This contract essentially says that you are dealing with borrowed money, and, For this reason, the brokerage organization has the right to interfere with its activities to protect its interests. Once registered, simply deposit on your account, and you are ready to trade immediately.

For most traders, the most difficult part of Forex trading is dealing with financial losses. It's not just a matter of pain and anguish, but it's also a fact that losses are usually the catalyst that leads traders to make their worst mistakes, which can result in even greater losses, creating a vicious spiral in which the account of the merchant turns. out of control.

It follows that a forex trader must have a strategy on how to manage the losses and be able to execute this adaptation strategy. There is no point in "knowing" that your losses are under control and how to keep them under control if you can not use knowledge. Your coping strategy must be real. You must understand the logic behind your knowledge of losses and believe the truth in faith.

Losses are inevitable

The loss of negotiations is inevitable; In fact, it is often more difficult to make money with strategies that try to ensure a very high victory rate. It's just the nature of how the market evolves.

Some traders follow a methodology that tries to reduce or even eliminate losses dramatically. There are only two methods to do it, and it is important to understand them perfectly:

- Adding to a lost negotiation, the belief that you were right in the original commercial entry, and that the timing was wrong. You can even add a larger amount to the next entry for easier recovery. The simple fact is that while this may work as a method, it's usually not ideal, and you'll usually get better results by simply accepting the first loss and closing the trade rather than attempting a "bailout." After all, if your original stop was reached, why would the second exchange be better than the first?

- "Turn in the wind" and open a trade in the opposite direction. In fact, it does not prevent a loss; In fact, it crystallizes a loss by changing its net position. If you have 1 long lot then buy 2 short lots, you end up with 1 short liquid lot with a crystallized loss in this 1 lot.

There is one more particular thing you can do: do not close the lost trades and let them run against you more and more. If you do that, you will close your account.

Fortunately, until now, I've convinced you that you have to accept a losing business. If I have not done so, please go back and read and re-read it until you are convinced. If you are not convinced, write to me and explain your reasons: I hope to convince you by email!

Know how many losses you can tolerate

If you have accepted, lost trades, and risk losing (called "downgrades"), you must decide how psychologically you can tolerate losing without losing your courage. To do this, you must have an honest conversation with yourself. You might think that you could handle something like a withdrawal of

50% on your trading account, but in reality, you do can not possibly manage 25% when it actually occurs. Try to visualize what's going on, close your eyes, and put yourself there.

Another second thing to consider is that as any reduction in your account increases, the amount you need to recover to get the amount you started increases. For example, if you lose 10%, you will need to increase the remaining 90% by 11.11% just to recover the original 100%. When you arrive at a very low 50% draw, you must earn 100% just to return to the original 100%. It is a bitter truth that the deeper your losses are, the harder it will be to get back to where you started.

After considering this, on the other hand, it is also true that the less risk you have, the less you will earn when trading is favorable.

Use a trading method that you really believe in.

After you are sure of the maximum loss you can tolerate, it is necessary that any method you use to decide when to go in and out of a trade and what to negotiate is a good method that generates a positive "wait." This means that in a large business sample, he earns more money than he loses.

You must believe that it is a lucrative method and also submit it to a functional test over several years of historical data.

This is important because when you hit an inevitable losing streak, you have the courage to continue. If you do not do it and stop trading, nor lose courage and excessive trading, you will lose the winning sequence after the losing sequence.

Another benefit of a backward test is that you can use a long-term backtest to determine the worst drawdown and the number of consecutive missed transactions. You can use it to make sure you can survive stretch marks lost. For instance, if the worst performance of your strategy in the last 10 years and thousands of transactions have lost 50 consecutive transactions and the maximum withdrawal you think you can tolerate is 25%, this suggests that if you risk 0, 50% of your capital per transaction, you probably suffer a downward revision over the next 10 years. If you reduce the risk by 0.25% per transaction, you reduce the probability of this depth of reduction.

You should also use a fractional share risk management system, which gives you greater peace of mind knowing that there is a buffer to reduce total losses. You can also decide that if you have a withdrawal much worse than the last 10 years, you will stop trading and reconsider your strategy.

Catastrophic losses

Sometimes events happen on the market to trigger price movements that are so large and so violent that even if you use a stop loss, your broker will not (or pretend not to be able to) execute it. This means that when the shutdown is finally triggered, you may experience much larger losses than you expected. The evolution of the Swiss franc 2015 is a good example. The Brexit vote last week is a much milder example.

You can avoid this problem by not negotiating any currency that central banks adopt the policy of swimming against the market, attaching the value to another currency, and not being in a position immediately before the high risk of something planned, like a referendum.

Peace of mind will help you cope

After taking these steps, you can be sure to risk money on transactions in the settings you set. You'll know pretty much what percentage of deals they tend to lose, how long the tracks tend to be, and, most importantly, ultimately, they tend to go ahead. At this point, you must accept that lost trades are natural and are just necessary sacrifices that you must make to the market to make money: a "cost to do business."

4 STAGES OF LOSS IN FOREX TRADE

I have already mentioned that loss is as much a part of negotiations as a victory. After all, forex trading is usually a game of zero-sum . Someone is definitely on the other side of your job, and it's only a matter of time before you get on the wrong side.

But while this is part of the overall bargaining process, losing is something that many traders - both beginners and professionals - are struggling with.

Losing in a game where absolute nothing is at stake is difficult enough, what else when there is real money for which you worked hard is involved?

I believe that the main reason for the difficulty in managing losses is the lack of understanding of their nature and impact on business psychology rather than actual psychological problems.

In this book, I would like to address this lack of knowledge with loss. I will talk about the four stages of currency loss, namely, denial, rationalization, depression, and acceptance.

Do you think the terms are familiar? They should because they are similar to the four stages of grief. Note that they are applied differently in the forex.

Knowing the four steps, I hope you are better able to handle trading losses.

Step 1: denial

The first step of the loss allows you to deal with the loss of transactions.

At this point, you deny to yourself and others that your trading idea was wrong and that the loss was not your fault. Reasons like "I stopped hunting" and "I do not really care about this job" are commonly used. There is nothing wrong with feeling this, especially if you are young. It's a way to mitigate the blow to your ego, survive the loss, and move on.

Step 2: Streamlining

After the rejection phase, you streamline your trading setup. This is the moment when you point out everything that is right in your business idea and does not even think about what you have done wrong.

You cite the relevance of your trading plan, your profit target, your stop loss, and your point of entry, but you are totally unaware that you have actually lost your trading and made a mistake somewhere.

Step 3: Depression

At this point, you have examined all the possible external explanations for your loss. You then turn inward and contemplate on the idea that the loss was entirely caused by your own action.

While it is reasonable to take responsibility for your loss, blaming yourself too much can hurt your career in the market if you constantly doubt yourself.

You may ask yourself, "Is forex trading really for me?" And "Why continue?" You can even withdraw from the company if you do not find enough reasons to keep moving.

Anyone who has experienced this kind of doubt can attest that the longer the defeat sequence, the more intense the feeling of despair. Some even think of pursuing other opportunities and giving up forex trading altogether!

Step 4: Acceptance

At this point, you begin to understand that it is unhealthy to blame you for everything that went wrong.

Even if you have accepted that the loss was partly your fault, you are also aware that the foreign exchange market is a wild and wild animal and that there are many factors of the market out of your control.

Let me clarify, however, that acceptance does not simply mean that the loss is good. In fact, acceptance is more about aligning with reality and realizing that loss can not be undone.

When you reach this level, you accept that you have made mistakes, but there are also things that you can not control.

Some even say that acceptance is a mixture of rationalization and depression when you combine the two before you can continue.

After everything, it's essential to remember that you can never really reverse what has been lost, but you can catch up with it.

One obvious technique to do this is to have a winning job and recover financially, but you can also recover mentally.

You can make improvements to your trading strategy, exercise better risk management, or simply discover how to better manage your losses.

Instead of denying the loss, you have to move forward, adapt, and grow.

BOUNCING BACK AFTER A BIG TRADING LOSS

Whether it's a technological collapse, a lack of discipline, or simply a continuous flight of commercial capital, almost all traders will face a major loss (or many) in their careers. How to recover after a big loss is not complex; This can be done in a few simple steps. The hard part is to repair the mental damage caused, especially the damage to the trust.

While overconfidence is blinding, successful traders do not exchange fear because fear is also blinding. This level of trust in which you see the market for what it is intervenes whenever there is an opportunity, reduces your losses when they do not happen, and puts your hand when the conditions are not good - it is the trust that can be lost after a sequence of defeats.

After a series of losses or a big loss, you can start asking yourself, which leads to all the typical problems of many new traders, such as withdrawing too quickly from trading, holding them back for a long time, ignoring the scary trades to lose, or enter more trades than it should, in order to win winning trades. If you encounter these problems or experience a significant loss of capital, there are ways to get you back on track.

The day of your loss

Every trader has bad days. In general, never let a bad day cost more than you earn a profitable average day. If you win an average of $ 700 on the days of victory, do not miss a lot more on a bad day. Check the inconvenience.

A great loss causes all kinds of internal conflicts - the need for revenge, fear, anger, frustration, self-hatred, market hatred, and the list goes on. After a big loss, there is no way to negotiate with a clear head. There are more than 250 trading days a year, so there is no hurry to return; Today is not the day of return.

Accept responsibility

Maybe it was a few bad days, maybe it was your biggest personal loss of all time, or maybe it's a life-changing loss. In the latter case - faced with financial ruin - there is not much to do. Do not negotiate until the problem is solved. Once it is, you can proceed with the steps below, but not before. Do not treat a huge debt over your head with the intention of using it to abolish this debt; It's a lot of pressure and can lead to a worse situation.

If you have withdrawn your account, suffered a defeat sequence, or suffered a sudden loss, it's different. You are still in the game, just a little beat. Everyone loves a story back, and every professional who has been around for a while has one (or more). It does not matter if a surprise announcement has pushed the price beyond your stop loss or if a technological failure has made you lose your connection, and the market has evolved against you.

There is always an excuse for a lost job. Some are very good excuses, but as traders, we must finally accept all the risks. Until we accept responsibility for everything that happens to our requests, history will probably be repeated, and the same thing will happen again.

Accept responsibility and find out what could have been done differently. This will help reduce the chances of re-offending. It is also healthier than swallowing hostility and blaming others for their misfortunes. To blame others is to admit that you do not control your own trading, and if so, why are you trading? If you control your trading, you can correct it; If other people control your trading, you can not fix anything.

There's always something to do. This may involve changing markets, connecting backup data, stopping losses, and automatically submitting targets when an exchange is initiated, or you can configure your platform to settle your transactions if you reach a loss limit daily. The solution is there; You just need to discover it. The best way to find it is to admit that the loss is the result of something wrong, and then to take steps to correct it.

The correction of the specific problem causing the loss is the first step. There remains the question of trust. Even with the problem solved, your confidence may be low after a hard blow.

Reorient your concentration

When you started, you were probably too confident, but the market put you in its place. You have developed a healthy trust over time by building your trading system, testing and practicing it, and finally using it for real money trading. Trust is created by accomplishing difficult tasks and improving these tasks. In trading, our aim is to implement our trading plan. Trust is growing as we see positive results from this business plan.

After suffering from a big loss, get back to basics. Concentrate on the trading plan (with any adjustments made) and its implementation. Return to what attracted you to the business first: develop or learn a strategy that has always made money. Negotiation is difficult, so like and accept the challenge again. Many good times can make us lazy, and often a big loss wakes up. It is the market that informs us that we have gone astray.

Practice and regain confidence

After a big loss, confidence can below. This means that the mind may not be right to negotiate. Not having a clear mind can make you skip negotiations, panic (do not negotiate not to lose), or be too aggressive in trying to return to your old winning methods quickly. None of this is good. Go back and swap a demo account for a few days. If you lose, it will probably save you money. Since this is not real money, there is also less pressure on a demo account, so it is easier to concentrate on trading and not worry about the financial aspect.

Start small

A few winning days on the demo account will increase your confidence level and put you in a better mental space to re-enter the market with real money. After a sequence of defeats, start small; Do not go back to the same position size that you traded before. On the first day of return, negotiate a small position size. A winning day accompanied by a small position size will help build confidence, and you can increase the size of your position the next day. If you have a lost day, the loss with small position sizes is easier to manage than another day with the loss of full position sizes.

Come back to live to trade at a slow pace. If you're really upset, spend at least 2 to 5 days in simulation and when you return to the floor, start small and increase the size of the position when you have winning days. Regardless of winning a few days in a row, gradually increase the size of your position, so it takes about a week to return to the maximum size of your position. I saw people trying to resume live trading after a big loss, and they were not ready. They ended up losing more. Some forex traders repeat this cycle and never recover.

After negotiating larger position sizes, it's annoying to start with a small position size, but it's the best. Recover from a string of losses is back to basics and to work well a strategy, not make money. The money comes from implementing a good strategy. Demonstration trading and small trading allow you to focus on what's important so you can start building trust again. The money will come on its own without being forced.

The essential

If you have just suffered a big blow, stop trading for a few days. When you return, review your trading plan and trading problems and solve the problem and make the necessary changes to the trading plan. Then redeem a demo account for a few sessions to build trust. Just switch to live to trade after a few profitable days and look more like your old and successful one.

HOW MUCH CAN I EARN FOREX DAY TRADING?

Many people like to trade foreign currency on the foreign exchange market because it requires the least capital to start day trading. Foreign exchange trades 24 hours a day during the week and offers a lot of profit potential because of the leverage provided by foreign exchange brokers. Forex trading can be very volatile, and an inexperienced trader can lose substantial amounts.

The following scenario shows the potential of using a forex day trading strategy controlled by risk.

Forex Day Trading Risk Management

Every successful day forex trader manages his risks; This is one, if not the most crucial, of continued profitability.

For starters, you have to keep the risk in every job very small, and 1% or less is typical. This means that if you have a $ 3,000 account, you should not lose more than $ 30 in a single transaction. This may seem weak, but the losses increase and even a good trading strategy of a day will see loss sequences. The risk is managed using a stop-loss order.

Forex Day Trading Strategy

While a strategy can possibly have many elements and can be analyzed for profitability in a number of ways, a strategy is often categorized by its rate of return and its risk / reward ratio.

Win rate

Your win rate represents the number of transactions you earn in a given total number of transactions. Let's say you earn 55 trades out of 100; your win rate is 55%. While not mandatory, having a win rate of over 50% is ideal for most daily traders, and 55% is acceptable and achievable.

Risk/Reward

Risk / reward means how much capital is risky to make a certain profit. If a trader loses 10 pips to lose trades but earns 15 pips to win, he wins more winners than losers. This implies that even if the trader only earns 50% of his trade, he will be profitable. Therefore, winning more winning deals is also a strategic element that many forex traders strive for.

A higher business gain rate means more flexibility with your risk / reward, and a higher risk / reward means that your win rate may be lower, and you will still be profitable.

Hypothetical scenario

Suppose an operator has $ 5,000 inequity and a decent 55% success rate in their trades. They take the risk of only 1% of their capital or $ 50 per transaction. This is done using a stop-loss order. In this scenario, a stop-loss order is placed at 5 pips from the entry price and a goal at 8 pips.

This implies that the potential reward for each transaction is 1.6 times higher than the risk (8/5). Remember, you want the winners to be bigger than the losers.

While trading a currency pair for two hours during an active hour of the day, it is usually possible to perform about five round transactions (the round includes the inputs and outputs) using the above parameters. If there are twenty trading days in a month, the trader will make 100 trades on average in a month.

Trading Leverage

Forex brokers offer leverage up to 50: 1 (more in some countries). In this example, suppose the trader uses a 30: 1 leverage, as it is usually more than enough for forex day traders. Because the dealer has $ 5,000 and a leverage of 30: 1, he can take positions worth up to $ 150,000. The risk is always based on the original $ 5,000; This limits the risk to a small portion of the deposited capital.

Forex brokers generally do not charge a commission, but increase the gap between supply and purchase, making profitable trading more difficult. ECN brokers offer a very small gap, which facilitates profitable trading, but they typically charge about $ 2.50 for every $ 100,000 exchanged ($ 5 shifts).

Trading Currency Pairs

If you trade a currency pair like GBP / USD daily, you can risk $ 50 on each transaction, and each move pip is worth $ 10 with a standard lot (100,000 currency units). Therefore, you can take a position on a standard lot with a 5 pip stop-loss order, which will keep the risk of loss at $ 50 in trading. It also means that a winning offer is worth $ 80 (8 pips x $ 10).

This evaluation can show how much a forex day trader could earn in a month by performing 100 trades:

- 55 profitable trades: 55 x $ 80 = $ 4,400
- 45 trades were losing: 45 x ($ 50) = ($ 2250)

Gross profit is $ 4400 - $ 2250 = $ 2150 if there are no commissions (the rate of gain would probably be lower)

Net income is $ 2150 - $ 500 = $ 1650 if you use a commission broker (the rate of profit would be higher)

Assuming a net income of $ 1,650, this month's account yield is 33% ($ 1,650 / $ 5,000). It may seem very high, and it's a very good return. See Improvements below to see how this feedback could be affected.

Larger loss than expected

It will not always be possible to find five good morning trades every day, especially when the market moves very slowly for long periods.

Slippage is an inevitable part of the trade. This results in a larger loss than expected, even when using a stop-loss order. It is common in very fast markets.

To explain the slippage in the calculation of your potential profit, reduce the net profit by 10% (this is a high estimate of slippage, assuming you avoid publishing large amounts of economic data). This would reduce the potential for net earnings generated by its trading capital from $ 5,000 to $ 1,485 per month.

You can adjust the above scenario based on your typical stop loss and goal, capital, slippage, win rate, position size, and commission parameters.

Conclusion

This simple risk control strategy says that with a 55% gain rate and win more winners than losing trades, you can earn returns of up to 20% per month with Forex Day Trading. Most traders should not expect to earn much; Although it sounds simple, it's actually harder.

Still, with a decent win rate and a risk / reward ratio, a dedicated day trader with a decent strategy can earn between 5% and 15% per month through leverage. Remember that you do not need a lot of capital to start with; Usually $ 500 to $ 1,000.

WHAT WILL IT TAKE TO MAKE $15,000 PER MONTH CURRENCY TRADING?

To make such a large profit per month, you must have an initial account of at least $ **33,000** (Analysis later). Many traders asked if they could earn $ 15,000 a month with a starting $ 10,000 account.

This is a big question. Many novice traders who are trying to make a lot of money exchanging currency fall into the trap of "unrealistic expectations" and I will take this opportunity to show you what I mean.

The foreign exchange trade has received a lot of attention over the years because of all the wonderful benefits it offers, especially accessibility and turnover in particular. You have undoubtedly read (or heard about) people who produce five or even six issues per month in this market.

Well, let's take a glance at what it really means to earn 5 digits in the fx currency market. $ 500 a day equals $ 15,000 a month. So, mostly, what you are really asking is how to double your money at least until the first month.

Let 's analyze again and see if it will work...

ANALYSIS

Let's suppose that you decide to make a trade a day (thus 20 trades for the month) to meet your target of $ 500 per day. Also, with $ 10,000 of starting capital, it is best to start with a mini-account (compared to a standard account). Now, on a mini account, each mini-batch generates $ 1 per pip captured (on average). Of course, it varies with currency pairs, but we'll assume it's $ 1 for that analysis. Now, at $ 1 / pip captured, you will need to capture 500 pips per day.

Ask yourself: is this realistic?

This is, unfortunately, not the case. And if you try to do it, you take too much risk to justify it in the first place. This leaves you with another alternative: increase the number of mini lots traded each day to increase your net gain per pip captured. You will reduce the number of pips you will need to capture daily.

Here are some possibilities:

- 2 mini lots - 250 pips required
- 5 mini lots - 100 pips required
- 7 mini-lots - 70 pips required (approximately)
- 10 mini lots - 50 pips required

Looking at these estimates above, 50 to 70 pips / day seem a better goal. Succinctly put, I think it's possible to capture 50-70 pips / day in this market, realistically, against 500 pip per day.

Now, I'm not saying that it's not possible to get 100 pips / day or even 500 pips (especially on days when there's a key ad). Plus, money changers are constantly coming in and out of this market, taking 1, 2, or 5 to 10 pips at once and doing it all day ... Your daily pips are sure to increase. But still, when you look at the ups and downs of a typical day in the major markets, you will find that even though the markets tend to be quite large, it is still worth keeping. And bear in mind, there will be days when you seek bargaining and simply will not find opportunities. Stupid traders forget it, which is very dangerous because they end up seeing what they want to see, all because they have a daily service goal (like 500 pips / day). Do you see where I'm coming from? Realistic expectations help you negotiate better, which preserves your capital in the long run. Needless to say, preserving capital means being able to make a profit in the future because it keeps you in the game longer. Trust me!

Let's go back to the analysis ...

So, let ' say's we are confident that we can find 70 pips / day of trading of the euro and the pound. We sell 7 mini lots, which means:

$ 7 profit / pip captured if the market favors us

... OR ...

$ 7 loss per pip if the trade turns against us.

Well, now we have to look at the risk. If you work at a ratio of 1: 1.5 (aiming to earn $ 1.50 for every $ 1.00 risky), you risk about $ 330 / swap (or 47 pips). About $ 500 is about 1.5 times the $ 330 (I use round numbers here instead of real numbers for simplicity). In 47 pips at risk (ex: in creating stop losses, which are 47 pips, I feel really comfortable because ' enough room for the market to move before I get stopped prematurely - so that looks good). The next point I should address is the percentage of risk I would take to make such a trade. In other words, if I ended up losing $ 330 in this business (instead of earning $ 500), what% of my business capital would be lost (or written off)? It turns out that $ 330 represents a capital loss of 3.3%, and it's not good. At this rate, my whole account would be exhausted in just 30 operations! It's a bad sign and a red flag that should immediately stop any trade.

Let go back to the original question now ...

You want to earn $ 500 a day with your $ 10,000 capital, but that would be very risky. You would need:

- Increase your capital or
- Try to earn less each day

If you're wondering, a loss of $ 330 represents 2.2% of $ 15,000 and about 1.7% of $ 20,000. In other words, you would need at least $ 20,000 on your account to justify the type of trading you intend to do (to my humble and conservative opinion, I had developed by blowing up my own account when I started). And just to shake your feathers a little more ... 1.7% is way too high for my taste. I would not exceed 1%, which represents an initial account of at least **$ 33,000.**

Yes, you read correctly: you need a good amount of money to really earn decent money in the foreign exchange market.

Make the accounts with $ 250 / day of profits or up to $ 350 and see how your risk levels are changing. If you are in the range of 1% to 2% (depending on your own risk tolerance), you'll have a better plan (assuming you're ready to earn $ 350 / day or up to $ 250 / day instead of $ 25). 500 - for now) . I would say that this is not a bad place to start!

CHAPTER TEN – STRATEGIES TO CREATE PASSIVE INCOME WITH CRYPTOCURRENCIES

If you're looking for more ways to potentially improve your cryptocurrency revenue, this chapter is for you. As cryptocurrency proliferates in the digital world, more than ever, there are many ways, aside from mining and currency preservation, to earn passive income from your investments.

So, if you have an interest in more than just hanging on to your chips and want to see your investments grow, read on. There are some options available, so I'm sure you'll find one that meets your encryption needs and fits your investment capacity.

This book examines ways to increase your encryption gains by taking advantage of your current challenges and making smarter investments in hardware that supports the distribution networks in which your currencies operate. Let's be honest; mining is not a possibility conceivable for most of us. However, there are many less capital and time-consuming ways to increase your encryption richness.

Here you will acquire the basic information you require to understand how to increase your stakes. This is the appropriate place to start before you do more research on the right method for you and your investment capabilities.

This chapter follows the following ways to increase your encryption gains passively.

- Run a Lightning Node: for the technical expert
- Foreign currency loan: margin trading and foreign currency lending
- Airdrops, Forks, and Buybacks
- EOS systems
    1. EOS dApp
    2. Ethereum dApps
- Staking cryptocurrency and proof of stake
- Masternodes Cryptocurrency

PASSIVE V. SORTA-PASSIVE

This chapter will focus on ways liabilities earn income in the cryptographic world, particularly on ways of your interest in your current issues. Most include participating in strengthening the decentralized network , or wagering their own chips and gaining interest in their current holdings.

Some of these investment strategies definitely need more commitment than others. Whatever your decision, make the decision based on your present comfort level and what fits your budget.

Remember, the higher the risk, the higher your potential rewards. Still, I'm always in favor of doing your homework and knowing what kind of options there are.

Here are 7 viable ways to potentially increase your earnings while you Hodl (hold on to your coins for Dear Life).

RUNNING A LIGHTING NODE

Layer 1 and Layer 2

In Blockchain Basics, Daniel Drescher describes the blockchain as a two-tier software system; *Application* and *implementation*:

> • Layer 1 is the application layer. This layer is responsible for all the components intended for the user. These are the things you use when interacting with your crypto-currencies.
> • Layer 2 of the deployment layer is the physical technology and design that makes the application work; These are things like the protocols and the code that run the program.

The lightning network refers to the payment protocol "Layer 2". This network runs on a cryptocurrency based on the blockchain (such as Bitcoin). In a way, it is excess to the blockchain. And by using Lightning networks, transactions are done much faster.

Lightning networks allow encryption micropayments to run on a bidirectional payment channel. In contrast, typical transactions are one-way; When Alice sends Bitcoin to Bob, it means that Bob can not use the same channel to send or receive funds from Alice.

But here's the problem: for bidirectional channels to work, our hypothetical users, Alice and Bob, must accept the deal before the transaction can be confirmed. Then, when opening a transaction, both must confirm the number of Bitcoins each will deposit on the same channel.

Join the Lightning Network

Lightning networks use a flexible fork such as Segregated Witness or SegWit. A SegWit flexible fork is used to provide flexible transactions. SegWit is used in the Bitcoin Layer 1 blockchain, which is a smooth modification of the cryptocurrency bitcoin transaction format.

A smooth range divides the transaction into two segments; This deletes the signature or, more specifically, the unlocking signature (or "cookie data"). This actually does two separate transactions, where the original part is separated from the end of the script structure.

In doing so, the original section contains the sender and recipient data, and the new "witness" structure contains scripts and signatures. The "control" segment is counted as one-quarter of its actual size, while the original data segment is counted typically. And so, the trading can move faster because it is actually moved to pieces.

Lower Fees using Lightning

So why is this a great way to generate passive income? Because it is a partial answer to the problems of scalability and fluctuation of transaction rates. The lightning rod   makes money   by processing transactions; many transactions, quickly.

This not only speeds up the transactions but over time, the Lightning network charges should also reduce Bitcoin transaction fees. Indeed, when transactions are faster, easier, and cheaper, this solves some of the current scalability issues facing distributed networks.

Transaction costs are proportional to the time the funds are retained and how long they take to process a specific route í is the network. The rate also affected by high traffic on the network. But lightning technology allows for many transactions to be treated on one single blockchain transaction.

Moreover, as it is now, it is not financially viable to send Bitcoin micropayments. However, with cheaper rates and faster transactions, the scalability of micropayments will facilitate most of the system.

Because lightning networks act as a soft fork, they create more malleability than a Bitcoin transaction. The Bitcoin script was intentionally designed with the original limitations in place. These limitations prevent the involuntary malleability of transactions.

Invest in lightning

Although Lightning Networks nodes do not offer significant immediate returns, they offer transaction fees. And, of course, the market will need them more in the very near future.

Here is a conclusion of some of the challenges that Lightning Networks is helping to improve, described by Poon and Dryja:

- Almost instant transactions make the payment of small purchases via Bitcoin feasible and not revocable.
- Reduce the need for cold storage portfolios (offline storage), allowing you to make large payments in and out of business quickly. It could also potentially reduce the risk of theft and third-party intervention.
- Third-party custodians would no longer be required for micropayments. Bitcoin blockchain rates are currently too high to accept micropayments.
- Move oversize and time-sensitive channel calculations to improve the rate of smart financial and escrow deals.

COIN LENDING

Coin lending is a totally passive way to obtain cryptographic funds and increase your investments. The best way to participate in foreign currency loans is probably to set up automated loans on an exchange platform. Coinlend offers a fully automated system in which the IA manages and coordinates loans of all currencies in this exchange.

Letting the system manage the loans for you is easily the most effective and efficient way to lend. The more funds you have for loan swaps, the more your automated system will work for you, and the more you will earn passive income. But it also means keeping a large amount of stock market encryption, which you should also consider when evaluating your risk appetite.

While bots do most of the work, the user controls the loan settings. Thus, you can define the duration and value of your loans. Loans can range from a few days to several months and also their size; It all depends on your passive income.

Bots for rent

How do your coins earn money?

Automated encryption exchanges allow you to optimize margin trading. Margin trading means using funds borrowed from a broker (or stock exchange) to exchange your cryptocurrency. The funds are used as a guaranteed wallet. The pieces are ã the BORROWED made profits for traders by changes to interfaces like Bitfinex and Poloniex.

Although there are several variables to take into account, including which coins to lend, the amount of the loan, and the duration, it is possible to earn 2% per day lending coins. Higher loan rates occur during parachuting or forks, as an unusually large number of traders want to reduce assets.

Airdrops, Forks, Burns, and Buybacks:

Taking advantage of airdrops, forks, burns, and redemptions is probably the most passive way to earn on your investments.

While these opportunities offer real benefits, they require a little more chance from the investor than from actual experience. But you can increase the chances of benefiting from it. To do this, you must absolutely follow the activity in the world of cryptocurrencies and monitor your stocks. If you know an air launch, it's a good way to increase your income in a very short time.

If you're ready to do your homework, it's an easy way to enjoy being in the right place at the right time. Here's how they work; Projects that create protocol-level (second) applications are more likely to offer drops. In this case, you will find more parachutes from protocol-level crypto-currencies like Ethereum, EOS, and Stellar.

What exactly is this? And how can you make most of these opportunities?

Air Drops

An air stream is a widespread distribution of a token or coin of cryptocurrency, which usually gives current coin holders a direct blow to the wallet. Those - are used primarily to draw attention to them and new followers. The amount you can potentially receive is usually directly proportional to your current issues.

But if you realize that the fall is early, you may have a chance to take advantage of the fall. This is part of the interest of an air-launch, to attract attention and encourage others to adopt a native token. These purchases are free as long as you already have the currency.

However, parachuting is not something you can rely on regularly to increase your income.

The Bitcoin cash, which is a fork of Bitcoin blockchain of origin, held one of the most remarkable scenes of all time. This took place in August 2017 and has resulted in owners' will be rivers of the original Bitcoin has the same amount of Bitcoins Bitcoin and Cash. Both have lasted, and Bitcoin Cash is among the most traded currencies on stock exchanges.

forks

Although forks can be lucrative, bands are also a much less reliable way to earn passive income than lending coins or running Lightning networks. Forks can be considered a bank error in your favor . Here is what happens; If a blockchain is detached from the main chain, sometimes this new fork creates an opportunity for a holder to obtain a proportionality (or comparable) to his assets in the new blockchain fork.

Again, the forks are excellent when they work for you, but you can not count on them as a stable way to passively develop an investment portfolio.

Burns and Buybacks

Burns and buybacks, like airdrops, are quite variable. But again, you may be lucky and miss to admit that in any investment, hopefully, do never wrong. Sometimes burns and redemptions can mean that the creator of a cryptocurrency buys his native token.

Redemptions are usually organized to burn part of the room. This is when a firm takes a certain amount of its currency. Creators send this currency to an address without a private key, which means that no one can access the currency. It is metaphorically called "burning" because money is artificially eliminated in an effort to control inflation.

Engraving is done to create a shortage because it eliminates part of the circulating currency in order to increase the value of the remaining currency. This can be a successful measure as it eliminates the problems of over-circulation and deflation. And in general, the value of the cryptocurrency you own should increase.

Again, you will need to keep cryptocurrency in your own personal or cold storage portfolio to be the complete recipient of the fork and parachute benefit. If your funds are held in a purse, she will likely receive the funds. So make sure to read the fine print.

As said earlier, these are not the best ways to earn a passive income simply because they look more like unexpected profits than a very complex strategy. But what you can do is keep the pair from advancing their investments, which, frankly, is good advice for all of us. And if you can enjoy a fall or a redemption, why not hit while the iron is hot!

Participate in EOS dApps

You can also get passive income on the Ethereum platform simply by betting your own chips. This allows other users to use the different Ethernet applications. And with you betting your own chips, you can earn some interest.

What exactly is happening here, you may be wondering. Let's take a look at the functioning of decentralized applications taken in load by EOS Dapps or Ethereum, and why you can bet your chips on EOS Dapps .

What is EOS dApps

EOS is an abbreviation for Ethereum operating applications or Ethereum operating systems. These dApps are created on the Ethereum blockchain and work on the decentralized network. They are more flexible applications and therefore do not suffer from the same transaction scalability that other blocks of channels and platforms - forms of decentralized networks such as Bitcoin.

Ethereum is best known for its decentralized applications rather than for the value of its native token. Ethereum is still the second major valuable cryptocurrency on the market today. And Ethereum's original coin offer is the most successful ICO so far. More than $ 4.1 billion was raised between June 2017 and June 2018.

To launch dApps on the EOS platform, you need your native token, Ether. Using the open platform of EOS, technology developers can create their own decentralized applications, called dApps. These dApps are executed using intelligent contracts, which are simply automated contracts that have been written in a compatible programming language.

EOSDivdends displays dApps with which you can earn dividends in EOS.

EOS and passive gains

This passive income method requires an investment in your equipment because you will not necessarily be able to use your personal computer. To participate in the splitting of your chips into EOS dApps, you will need a CPU and a RAM.

You must also have EOS tokens to run the programs. Betting your chips is a great way to earn a passive income because it allows you to earn interest. Indeed, the placement of your chips allows other people to use dApps. The DAPPS popular have to need Paris are for players like poker and play.

Once again, the interest you earn will depend on the number of chips you have and the scope of your loan. However, you can earn a daily interest in your chips.

But to make the most of the interest, you will need to buy the native App token, as not all of them necessarily work on Aether alone. Investing in new native chips is always a risk, so it's best to research and see which chips have been able to maintain their value for a reasonable period of time.

Participating in Ethereum dApps

The Dapps Ethereum as Golem, MakerDao, and Augur allow investors to get chips supporting the network. Ethereum dApps specifically has fewer active users. However, these dAs are a growing concern and can, therefore, become even more lucrative in the future.

In addition, if you already have Ether, participation in these lower performance dApps is only one set. Most importantly, the system relies on Ether to run dApps.

MakerDao provides an exceptional incentive to act as the necessary guardian to maintain the DAI token counter. The process can be fully automated for you. The bots then look for opportunities to arbitration encryption, which keeps the anchoring of DAI and accelerates the settlement when the ETH prices drop.

STAKING AND POS

Bets can be the most direct and passive way to make money on your encryption investments. Unlike the expectation of an unexpected crop of a jet of air or a buy-back, this method gives a much more predictable return on income potential. In addition, you do not have to invest in special equipment; you just need the parts you bet on to help manage the network.

What is staking?

Staking is part of what is known as PoS or "proof of implantation." PoS is   a consensus algorithm; the Buterin Ethereum is   a   big   fan   of   this method.

Therefore, "bet" means that you bet your coins as part of the network consensus to add new blocks to the blockchain in which you are trading.

Here is how it works. You can only bet up to the total amount of coins you have. Your currencies are used to validate new transactions on the platform. And although you can only bet as many coins as you have, the more coins you bet, the more power you have to validate transactions.

How does PoS work ?

PoS is essentially the opposite of PoW or Bitcoin mining. One of the problems of mining is that it is a kind of bet on the node that will succeed. With mining, the first node to resolve the complex algorithm and achieve the hash goal is the one that will be rewarded by the new Bitcoins. As a result, not only is mining extremely expensive, both informally and energetically, but real money investors do not necessarily have a role to play in mining.

But with the PoS protocol, the miners are the ones who have assets in digital currency. Therefore, betting your coins means participating in mining and consensus. The knot simply bets a number of coins in his wallet, creating a new block. The minor is randomly selected in the selection by other coin holders.

The amount you can bet and mine is directly proportional to your bets. As a result, if you have 10% of the total currency in circulation, your node can extract up to 10% of new block trades. This will earn you interest in the coins you bet. In general, there is also a period of maturity. Which means you have to bet your chips for a while before you can start winning rewards.

Benefits of Staking Coins

Placement of parts has several advantages for mining operators compared to PoW. Here are a few:

> • You do not need mining equipment to participate in the setting; The betting application is made from an electronic wallet.
> • Those who hold stakes are responsible for the validation of transactions. This has the potential to encourage good behavior because you what interested in maintaining the validity of blockchain and the currency in which it invests.

- PoS does not suffer the same type of depreciation as the ASIC hardware, which is the current standard for mining with PoW. The investment is in foreign currency and is not wasted on equipment expenses.
- In short, PoW is less expensive in terms of calculation and therefore does not require the same amount of energy that Bitcoin PoW requires from its pools, which is a huge hurdle that the Bitcoin blockchain must handle.
- Many PoS supporters, including Ethereum creator Vitalik Buterin, believe that betting is the solution to one of the cryptocurrency use and scalability problems.

But most importantly, for this chapter, bet chips is a great way to get a potential passive income from your crypto-investment. Essentially, by betting, the holder earns interest in everything he holds and is willing to bet. This amounts to earning interest on your savings account. Fortunately, it will be more profitable, and you will be paid in the same currency as the one you are betting on.

The use of PoS and coin issues is becoming more and more popular in the world of encryption. PoS is increasingly integrated with new currency consensus models. Again, the interest you earn will not be consistent across each currency or electronic wallet.

Winnings are based on a number of factors, including the value of the coin, the amount you own, and the duration of your bets.

Here are some crypto-currencies on which you can bet currencies, and you should spend time looking for if you are interested in betting:

- **DASH**: or digital money. This was the first coin to introduce bets on coins. It was created at the heart of Bitcoin but has made some improvements by adding PrivateSend and InstantSend resources.

- **NEO:** Platform participants can bet their currencies by linking currencies to a NEON wallet.
- **OkCash:** OkCash was founded in 2014 and is suitable for microtransactions.

MASTERNODES: MEDIUM PASSIVE INCOME

It is a little exaggerated to add masternodes to the list of "passive income." But you can say that after the initial masternode creation work, there is a lot more passive work to do.

The masternodes are expensive and take the time. However, if you can manage the capital to start your own, there is a significant return on investment potential.

Masternodes are complete nodes and encourage node operators to perform the basic consensus functions required to execute a blockchain. Masternodes exist to try to solve some of the problems of running complete nodes, mainly the cost of the equipment and the high energy demand.

Today, blockchain network management faces the challenges of rising costs, as well as the technical complexities of running a full-node computer. The result of these problems has been a reduction in computers with complete nodes.

With fewer complete nodes, the blockchain can not operate with maximum efficiency. This is a constant problem faced by crypto-currencies and blockchains in general, scalability and energy efficiency still need to be fully optimized.

The bottom line, though, is that running your typical complete node and blockchain consensus participation is not very profitable at the moment.

In addition, mining basins alone require a significant amount of energy. The cost of mining has resulted in a decrease in the total number of nodes and in the same way to the efficiency of the blockchain.

Running a masternode

Master nodes operate on a work - tested system because they act as complete nodes. It is also a warranty-based system designed to encourage the maintenance of the blockchain network base. However, running a master node is not a passive activity.

Masternodes are composed of servers that maintain the network of a blockchain. These nodes are responsible for specific services that allow minors can not do. Masternodes participate in the test of the consensus mechanism at work. The first crypto to make use of a masternode as part of its blockchain consensus mechanism was Darkcoin, which was later renamed DASH.

As a result, Masternodes also participate in betting. This means that a masternode uses similar protocols to implement protocol evidence. When staking tokens, a certain amount of chips is stuck in your network.

Risks and rewards

Again, running a masternode can be very lucrative. You can earn up to 10% interest per year by running a masternode. However, some warnings and costs must be taken seriously. In the meantime, we can probably label the masternode as a *mean passive* gain. But although they are much more expensive, masternodes can be a much more lucrative investment than direct bets.

Masternodes v. Staking

As expected, the potential for higher rewards also requires greater risk. Although masternodes are a very lucrative investment, and once you have them as a passive form of income, there are still several essential factors to consider.

If you are seriously considering increasing your investments in masternode or staking, here are some things to consider:

- If you want to take part effectively, you will need to maintain a diversified portfolio of currencies. Having holdings in various currencies can be a very good thing, but it also opens up more risks. The fact is that not all currencies on the market have power, so it's a bit of a gamble for everyone.

• To take part effectively in a masternode, you will need to have bigger stakes in the currencies you are betting on. Implementation tokens require only modest maintenance, although this is not the case with masternodes.

• Again, the bet has a very low cost and a modest return on investment. However, masternodes need a little more capital to make them work. You must have access to a dedicated server and cover the expenses associated with it.

• Staking is much less difficult technically and does not require any specific equipment. Alternatively, master nodes have a steeper learning curve and require much more technical knowledge.

• In short, gambling is a much more passive form of income than a masternode. Masternodes must be actively maintained and therefore require much more attention.

REVIEW

Now, I hope you understand that there are many ways to participate in the growing world of cryptocurrencies and many ways to increase your investments. As might be expected, some methods require more work than others.

Let's glance at some of the passive strategies we talked about:

Run a Lightning Node

- Lightning networks are a Layer 2 solution. They work as a complete node and make transactions faster and easier, as well as micropayment on the Bitcoin network.
- Lightning Networks offer cheaper rates and faster transactions. However, the scalability of micropayments will ease most of the system.
- Although Lightning Networks nodes do not offer significant immediate returns given the value they add to cryptocurrency networks; it makes sense that they will need more of them in the market as they become more valuable. popular. As such, network owners should see their yields increase as their use increases.

Coin Lending: margin trading and coin lending

- This is the easiest way to get passive income. All that is needed is to put your current reserves in service for trading and margin loans.
- The easiest way to take part is to set up automated loans on a trading platform like Coinlend. These systems are fully automated, and the AI manages and coordinates the loans of all currencies in this exchange.
- Using the automated system is the most effective and efficient way to lend, because of the more funds you have available for loan swaps, the more your automated system will work for you.
- So, let the bots run and make money!

Airdrops, Forks, and Buybacks

- Airdrops, forks, and buybacks require a bit of luck and a little knowledge. These unexpected gains have obvious benefits, but they require a little more luck for the investor.
- To benefit, follow the steps of your tokens and current commercial developments.
- It's a great way to potentially increase revenue in a very short time, which is very easy.
- Second-level / protocol applications have more frequent airdrops than others. This means that protocol-level crypto-currencies such as Ethereum, EOS, and Stellar tend to offer parachutes and forks more often than others.

EOS systems

- This passive income method requires investment and upgrading of your equipment. To participate in the splitting of your chips in EOS of APPs, you will need a computer with CPU and RAM.
- You must also have good EOS tokens to run programs, not just Ether, but also other native tokens.
- Placement of the chips allows you to gain interest by using your chips to perform other dApps. The DAPPS are typical for players like poker and play.

- The interest you get depends on the number of chips you have and the scope of your loan. However, you can earn a daily interest in your chips.
- To get the most out of your interest gain, you will need the native App token, which means some will inevitably work better than others.

Staking cryptocurrencies and Proof of Stake

- By betting, the holder earns interest in everything he holds and is willing to bet. This is like earning interest on your savings account. Hopefully, it will be more profitable, and you will be paid in the same currency as the one you are betting on.
- Betting can be the most direct and passive way to win your encryption investments actively; This method offers a much more predictable return. To bet, you must only have the coins you are betting on.
- The owner can bet the number of coins he owns; these coins are used to validate new transactions on the platform. You can only bet as many coins as you need. But the more coins you bet, the more power you have to validate transactions.
- Real gains are based on several factors; who understands the value of the coin, how much you hold, and how long you bet.

Masternodes and staking

- Master nodes operate on a work - tested system because they act as complete nodes. It's also a guarantee-based system, so the more you can invest, the more you can earn.

- The masternodes are responsible for enabling the Service ç specific e phage that miners n ã can it do and can participate in the consensus mechanism for the trial work.
- The first crypto to make use of a masternode as part of its blockchain consensus mechanism was Darkcoin, which was later renamed DASH.
- Masternodes participate in staking. Staking tokens mean that a certain amount of chips is stuck in your network.
- You can earn up to 10% interest per year by running a masternode. Masternodes are a much more lucrative investment than direct bets.

MANY WAYS OF EARNING

The bottom line is that if you wish to see your investments grow, you need to take a more practical approach to manage them. However, this is not necessarily bad news for cryptography enthusiasts. And there are easy ways that are much more passive than active.

Lightning Networks nodes and Masternodes may require a bit more investment. But if you already have a coin in a purse or platform, there is no reason not to gain interest in wagering your coins as soon as possible.

The decision you make is how much time you want to invest in increasing your cryptographic wealth and what level of risk is right for you.

If you want to dive and take passive encryption revenue seriously, we encourage you to take a closer look at masternodes and lightning networks. As I mentioned, none of these are proving to have very high returns in a short time. However, both offer secondary passive income.

More importantly, for now, both contribute to better encryption systems. So, if you have capital and knowledge, running a Lightning network or buying a master node will earn you more revenue over time and help improve the system.

Now, if you have lots of quality coins, it may be in your interest to lend coins, and if you are investing in EOS or Ethereum systems, bet your chips. This is by far the easiest method to use your assets. To take part, all you do is set up automated loans on a purse like Coinlend , and the bots will work to make money.

Finally, we have the unexpected gains of parachuting, burns, and buybacks. To make the most of these incredible lotteries that can increase your wealth, you need to have a diversified portfolio of crypto-currencies, a wallet, and keep control of your investments.

Conclusion

We've looked at ways to increase your encryption wealth from the most intelligent to the most passive. The methods we have discussed range from low-interest income to higher interest income.

Here is an examination of the passive income investing methods we discussed:

- **Run Lightning Node; Foreign currency loans: margin operations and foreign currency loans; Airdrops, Forks, and Buybacks; EOS systems; Currency Encryption and Proof of Participation; Cryptocurrency Masternodes**

- Remember, this is not investment advice. These are examples of ways you can increase your wealth. But, as I mentioned, it is essential to do your homework. Before investing in ICO or IEO, check what's going on under the hood. What works for one investor does not work for another.

All of these passive income approaches are in their infancy. This means that there is probably a lot to gain from being one of the first to adopt. However, it also means that we really do not know what will remain. All this to say that before you go to town to build your own mining area, see what a reasonable and achievable project for you is.

Finally, your income varies proportionally depending on what you are willing and able to invest, the methods and currencies you choose, and your business knowledge. I have omitted any solid prediction about the real gain potential for many of these passive methods simply because it will depend on a confluence of factors.

One of the key factors for successful passive income will be how you stay informed and stay calm in the face of the volatile encryption market. It's a gold rush! Some will get richer, and others will find nuggets in the sand. But you can not win if you do not play!